I0734731

Classic Chinese Love Tales

Translated from the original of
Georges Soulie de Morant

The original source of the stories appearing in this collection of Chinese love stories is the classic literature of China in the seventeenth century.

Library and Archives Canada Cataloguing in Publication

Soulié de Morant, G. (Georges), 1878-1955, translator
Classic Chinese love stories / translated from the original of Georges Soulie de Morant.

Originally published in 1935 under title, Chinese love tales.
Translation of seventeenth century classic Chinese literature.
Issued in print and electronic formats.

Chinese literature--Translations into English. I. Title.

PL2658.E8S68 2015 895.13'408 C2015-900761-5 C2015-900762-3

Published by Soul Care Publishing, Vancouver, Canada

Classic Chinese Love Stories includes some of the best classics from China. Written in a graceful and beautiful style, each story evokes images of overcoming love's obstacles, passion, and the endurance of tragedy. These stories are exceptional in literary merit.

About the Translator:

Georges Soulié de Morant (1878-1955) was a scholar-diplomat engaged in the French diplomatic service in China between 1901 and 1917, where he gained entrance to the highest circles of the Chinese society. Although his life's work was acupuncture, his literary output was voluminous and covered every aspect of Chinese culture. He was a man of great talent, and became the only European recognized as a Chinese doctor by the Chinese themselves.

TABLE OF CONTENTS

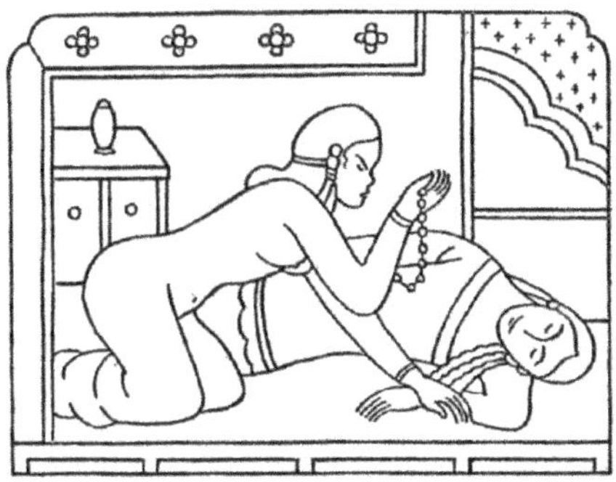

TU SHIH-NIANG, BEAUTIFUL COURTESAN

When there is a great peace
Under the gold cup of the sun
Joy reaches its flowering.

In the twentieth year of the period Wan-li, there came, among the thousands of students who gathered at Peking for the examinations, a certain Li, whose first name was Chia and his surname Ch'ien-hsi, or “Purified-a-thousand-times.” His family were from Shao-hsing fu in Chekiang; his father was Judge of the province of Kang-su; and Li himself was the eldest of three brothers. He had studied in the village school from childhood and, not having yet attained to literary rank, had come, according to custom, to present himself for examination at Peking. While in that city, he consorted, before his springtide, with the young libertines, the "willow twigs" of his country; and, in order to gain experience, frequented the theatres and music-halls. Thus he became acquainted with a famous singing girl called Tu, whose first name was Mei, or “Elegance.” As she was the tenth of her family, she was known at the theatre as Shih-niang, "The Tenth daughter." A delicate seduction diffused from her: her body was all grace and perfume. The twin arches of her brows held the black which is blue of distant mountains, and her eyes were as deep and bright as autumn lakes. Her face had the glory of the lotus, and her lips the glory of cherries. By what blunder of the gods had this piece of flawless jade fallen in the windy dust, among the flowers beneath the willow? When she was thirteen years old, Shih-niang had already "broken her claws." Now she was nineteen, and it would not be possible to enumerate the young Lords and Princes whose hearts she had besotted, whose thoughts she had set in a turmoil, whose family treasures she had swallowed without compunction. In the theatres, they had composed an epigram about her:

When Tu Shih-niang comes to a banquet
The guests drink a thousand great cups
Instead of a single small one.
When Tu Mei appears upon the stage
The actresses look like devils.

It must be said that never, in the young passions of his life, had Li Chia experienced the pain of beauty; but, when he saw Shih-niang, emotion was awakened in him, and the feelings of a flowering willow filled his breast. He himself was gifted with rare beauty, and a sweet and gentle nature. He spent his money recklessly, with an unbridled zeal for bestowing gifts. For this reason he held a double attraction for Shih- niang, who considered that falsehood and avarice were opposed to rectitude, and had also by this time made up her mind to return to a life of honor. She appreciated Li Chia's gentleness and generosity, and was drawn toward him. But he was afraid of his father and did not dare to marry her at once, as she wished.

Their love was not, on that account, any the less tender. In the joys of dawn and the pleasures of twilight they kept together as do husband and wife, and in their vows they compared their love with the Ocean or with the Mountain, recognizing no other vital motive. In truth:

Their tenderness was deeper than the sea
For it was past sounding,
Their love was as the mountains
But even higher.

Also, since Chia had been admitted to her favor, rich Lords and powerful Ministers were no longer permitted to see the girl's beauty. At first Li used to give large sums of money, so that the matron to whom Shih-niang belonged shrugged her shoulders and smiled. But the days went quickly, and the months too; and a year had passed. Chia's coffers had gradually become empty, and now his hand could no longer keep pace with his wishes. But the ancient ma-ma remained patient.

In the meanwhile the Judge had learned that his son was frequenting the theatre, and sent him repeated orders to return home. But Chia, who was infatuated, kept on delaying his departure until, hearing that his father was truly furious, he no longer dared to return. It was well said by the ancients: “As long as harmony endures there is unity; when harmony ceases, there is separation.”

Shih-niang's love was sincere, and her heart only burned the more for him whose hands were empty. The ma-ma frequently ordered her to send her lover away; then, seeing that the young girl was indifferent to her commands, she tried to exasperate Chia with stinging words, hoping thus to compel him to depart. But her visitor's nature was so gentle that his anger could not be provoked, and the only result was to make him more amiable in his behavior to the old woman, who in her impotence ended in reproaching Shih-niang:

“We who keep open doors must eat our visitors three times a day, and clothe ourselves with them. We lead out the departing guest by one door, but to receive a fresh one by another. When desire is excited under our roof, our silver and silks mount up like hills. But it is more than a year since this Li Chia began troubling your curtains, and now old patrons and new guests alike have discontinued their visiting. The spirit Chung-k'uci no longer comes to our door; nay, not the littlest devil. Therefore I am angry and humiliated. What will become of us, now that we have no trace of visitors?”

Shih-niang restrained herself with difficulty under these reproaches, and answered calmly:

“Young Lord Li did not come here with empty hands. He has paid us considerable sums of money.”

“It was so at one time; but it is now so no longer. Tell him to give me enough to pay for rice for the two of you.... Indeed, I have no luck! Most of the girls I buy claim all the silver, and hardly care whether their clients live or die. But now I have reared a white tiger who refuses riches, opens wide the door, and makes my old body bear the total burden. O miserable child! You wish to keep the poor for nothing. Where will you find clothes and food? Tell your beggar to be wise enough to give me a few ounces of silver. If you will not send him away, I shall sell you and look for another slave. That would be better for both of us.”

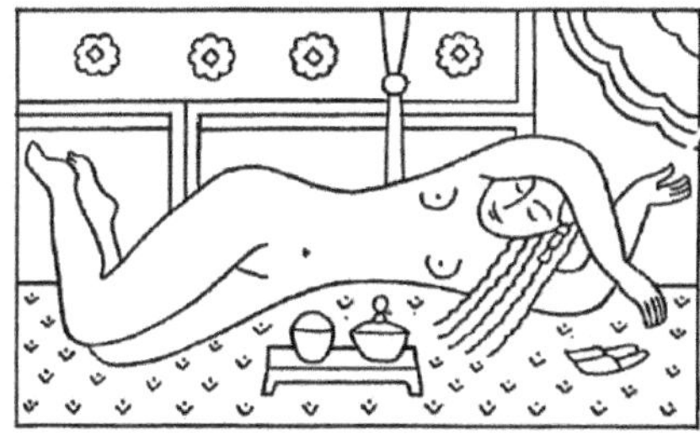

"Do you mean what you say?" asked the girl. "But you know that Li Chia has neither money nor clothes, and cannot procure any."

"I am not jesting," answered the old woman.

"Then how much must he give to take me away?"

"If any one else were in question, I should demand several thousand ounces. Alas! This beggar cannot pay them! So I shall be satisfied with three hundred ounces, with which to buy another 'tinted face.' If he brings them within three days, I will take the silver with my left hand and give the girl with my right. But after three days, it matters not at all to me that three times seven are twenty-one; Lord or no Lord, I shall beat out this young spark with my broom, and you must bear no grudge for it."

"In spite of all, he should be able to borrow three hundred ounces. But three days is too little; he will need ten."

"Ten days!" cried the other. "A hundred would be more like! Yet so be it. I will wait ten days."

"If he cannot get the money, he will not have the face to return. My only fear is that you will go back on your promise, if he does bring the three hundred ounces."

"I am nearly fifty-one years old," answered the ma-ma. "Ten times I have offered the great sacrifices. How should I dare not to keep my word? If you mistrust me, let us strike the palms of our hands together to fix the agreement. Nay, if I break my word, may I be changed into a pig or dog!"

That same evening, by the pillow-side, Shih-niang explained how her body might be re-bought, and Li Chia said:

“That would delight me, but how can I pay so much? My purse is as empty as if it had been washed.”

“Your slave has arranged all with the ma-ma. She requires three hundred ounces within ten days. Even if you have spent all that your family gave you for your journey, you have still some friends or relations from whom you can borrow. Then you will have me entirely to yourself, and I shall never again have to endure that woman's anger.”

“Since I became obsessed by our love, my friends and relations have ceased to recognize me. But perhaps, if I asked them to help me to pay for my journey home, I might make up the sum.”

In the morning, when he had arranged his hair and clothed himself, and was about to leave Shih-niang, she said to him:

“Do your uttermost, and come back to me with good news.”

He went to all his relations and friends, pretending that he was taking leave of them before his departure. They all congratulated him; but when he spoke of the expenses of the journey and asked for a loan, all, without exception, told him that they could do nothing. His friends knew the weakness of his character, and that he was besotted with love for some “Flower-in-the-Mist” or other. He had remained in Peking, up to that time, they knew, not daring to face his father's anger. Was this departure genuine, now, or but pretended? If he spent the borrowed money on ‘tinted faces,’ would not his father bear a grudge against those who lent it? The most he could get together was from ten to twenty ounces.

Ashamed of his failure after a full three days of endeavor, he did not dare to return to Shih-niang; yet, since he used to spend every night with his mistress, he had no other lodging. After the first evening, therefore, he went and asked shelter from his fellow-countryman, the very learned Liu Yu-ch'un. This man, seeing the growing sadness of the young man, at last ventured to question him, and learned his story and of his plan of marriage. Liu shook his head: "That is hardly possible. She is the most famous of all the singing girls. Who would be content with three hundred ounces for such a beauty? The old woman has conceived this method of sending you away, and Shih-niang, knowing that your hands are empty, asks you for this sum because she does not dare to tell you to leave her. If you offered the silver, she would laugh at you. It is a common trick. Do not trouble yourself further, but resign yourself to the breaking off of your relations with the girl."

Li Chia was speechless for a long time, shaken by his doubts, and Liu added:

"Make no mistake about it. If you show that you really mean to take your departure, many will help you. But as for your plan, you would need not ten days, but ten months to find three hundred ounces."

"Good Elder-Brother," answered Li, "your judgment is indeed profound."

But none the less he continued his vain search for three further days.

Shih-niang was most anxious when she did not see her lover" come back to her. She sent a little servant to look for him, and the child met Li by chance, and said:

"Lord, our Elder-Sister awaits you at the house."

In his shame, Li answered:

"I have no time to-day. To-morrow I will come to see her."

But the boy had been commanded to bring him back, and to die sooner than lose him, so he replied:

"It is the absolute wish of the Elder-Sister that you come with me."

Li could not refuse, and followed the messenger.

Once in Shih-niang's presence he stood still, sobbing mo-mo, mo-mo, without a word.

"How is our plan going?" she asked.

He only answered with a flood of tears; so she insisted:

"Can people have been so hard as to refuse three hundred ounces?"

Stifling his sobs, he answered with this verse:

It is easier to catch a tiger in the mountains
Than to move the world, with speech alone.

"I have gone about for these six days, and my hands are empty. Shame has kept me away from my perfumed companion, and it is only at her command that I have come back. I have tried my hardest. Alas! such is the spirit of the century."

"We will say nothing to the ma-ma. Let my Lord stay here for the night: his slave will propose another plan to him."

She served him with a meal and wine, and made him lie down. Then in the middle of the night she asked:

"If you cannot find three hundred ounces to free me, what are we to do?"

He wept without answering. Shih-niang waited until the fifth watch; then she drew from under her mattress a bag containing a hundred and fifty ounces in small silver, and said:

"This is my secret reserve. Since you cannot find the whole sum, I will give you half of it. That should help you; but we have only four days more. Above all, do not come too late!"

Astonished and overjoyed, he carried away the bag and went back to Liu, telling him what had happened and showing him the money. Liu exclaimed:

"Surely this woman has a loyal heart! Since she acts so, she must not be allowed to suffer. I am going to act as mediator in your marriage."

Leaving Li in his house, he went himself to ask for loans on all sides. In two days he had amassed a hundred and fifty ounces. He gave them to the young man, saying:

"I have stood guarantor for you, for I am deeply touched by Shih-niang's sentiment."

Li took the silver, as delighted as if the money had fallen from the sky, and ran to see his mistress. It was the ninth day. She asked him: "Has it been very difficult? Have you found the hundred and fifty ounces?"

He then told her what Liu had done; and both, rejoicing, spent a night of pleasure. Next day she said to him:

"When this money is paid, I must follow my Lord. But we have made no preparation for the boats and conveyances of our journey. I have borrowed twenty ounces from my friends. My Lord may take them for travelling expenses."

In his uneasiness concerning these expenses, he had not dared to speak of them. He took the money, and was full of joy.

At that moment there was a knock on the door, and the old woman entered, saying:

"This is the tenth day."

"I thank the ma-ma for recalling the fact to us," he answered. "I was on the point of paying her a visit."

And, taking up the bag, he poured the three hundred ounces on to the table. The old woman had not supposed he could succeed.

She changed color, and seemed on the point of gainsaying her word. So Shih-niang said: "I have stayed in your house for a long time, and have brought in several thousands of ounces. To-day I am marrying. If you do not keep your word, I shall commit suicide before you, and you will lose the money and the girl."

The old woman could find no words to express her feeling. She took the money in silence, and finally muttered:

"If you mean to go away, you go now. But you shall take none of your clothes or jewels with you."

Hustling the two young people along, she led them through the door and shot the bolt.

It was then the ninth moon, and the weather was cold. Shih-niang had but just risen from bed, and was not dressed; nor was her hair done. Yet she saluted the ma-ma with two genuflexions. Li Chia shook his two hands joined together. Thus the married pair left that not too pleasant old woman:

Even as a carp escapes the metal hook,
Flirts its tail and shakes its head
And returns not.

In front of the door Li Chia said to his mistress:

"Wait a moment! I will call a little palankeen to take you to the house of Liu."

She answered:

"In this very court are my friends, my sisters, who have always been in sympathy with me.

"I must take leave of them; and I cannot neglect to thank them for the money they have lent me."

Accompanied by her Lord, she went to each pavilion to greet her friends. Now, one of them, Yuch-lang, was a very close friend of Shih-niang, so, seeing that she had not done her hair, she led her to her own toilet-table, and ran to call another friend, Hsu Su-Su. Then she took from her coffers many ornaments of king-fisher leather and bracelets and jasper pins, even embroidered robes and girdles ornamented with phoenix. She gave them to Shih-niang, overcoming her with gratitude.

She also ordered a feast of congratulation, to which all their friends were invited, and finally, at the end of day, offered the pair a bed for the night.

When she was alone with Li Chia, Shih-niang asked:

"Where shall we go when we have left the capital? 'Has my Lord made a decision on this point?"

"My father," he answered, "is still angry with me. If, in addition, he learns that I have married my little sweetheart and that I am coming back with her, he will doubtless be carried quite away by rage. I have not found a satisfactory plan."

"Your father has feelings from Heaven. He could not break completely with you. Would it not be better for us to go to him, and to keep to our boat while you pray your friends to go and ask for a harmonious reconciliation? After that, leading your slave, you may re-enter your dwelling in peace."

"That is an excellent plan," he answered.

Next day they thanked Yuch-lang again, and went to the house of Liu. On seeing the learned man, Shih-niang knelt down to express her gratitude to him, saying:

"Later we may both know how to return your kindness."

Liu hastened to answer, according to the polite formality:

"Your admirable sentiment far exceeds my most poor action. You are a heroine among women. Why, then, do you hang such words to your teeth?"

All day the three of them drank wine of joy. Then the pair chose a suitable day for their journey, and obtained horses and palankeens. When the time for their departure drew near, Yuch-lang, Hsu-Su, and all those friends came to bear the couple company. Yuch-lang sent her servants to bring a metal casket, furnished with a golden lock, and gave it to Shih-niang, who placed it in her palankeen without opening it.

The porters and servants urged the travelers forward, and they started. Liu and the beautiful women escorted them as far as the other side of the Ch'ung-wen gate, and there they drank a last cup together. They separated with tears.

When they reached the river Lu, Li Chia and Shih-niang abandoned the land way and hired a cabin in a large junk which was going to Kua-chow. After he had paid their passage in advance, there was only a single piece of bronze left in Li Chia's bag; the twenty ounces which Shih-niang had given him had vanished as if they had never been. The young man had not been able to avoid giving certain presents, and he had also bought blankets and other necessities for the journey. Sadly he asked himself what was to be done, but she said to him:

"My Lord may cease to disturb himself. Our friends have given yet more help."

She opened her metal casket, while he looked on in shame. She took out a red silk bag and put it on the table, bidding him open it. He found the bag heavy; for, in fact, it contained fifty ounces of silver. Shih-niang had already shut the casket again, without saying what further was in it; now she said smilingly:

"Have not our sisters the most desirable instinct? They did not wish us to have any difficulty on our journey, and in this way they enable us to cross mountains and rivers."

Li Chia exclaimed in his delight and surprise:

"If I had not met such generosity, I should have had no choice but to wander, and at last to die without burial. Even when my hair turns white, I shall not forget such virtue and such friendship."

And he shed tears of emotion, until Shih-niang consoled him by diverting his thoughts.

Some days later they reached Kua-chow, where the big junk stopped. But Li Chia was now able to hire a smaller vessel for themselves alone, and in this he stowed their baggage. On the morrow they were to travel across the great river.

* * *

It was then the second quarter of the second month of winter. The moon shone like water. The pair were sitting on the deck of the junk, and the boy said:

"Since we left the capital we have not been able to talk freely, because we were in a cabin and our neighbors could hear us. Now we are alone on our own junk. Also, we have left the cold of the North and will to-morrow be on the south side of the river. Is it not a fitting time to drink and rejoice, so as to forget our former sorrows? You to whom I owe so much, what do you say?"

"It is now long since your slave was deprived of little pleasantries and laughters, and she had the same sentiment .as yourself. Your words prove that we have but one soul."

They brought wine on deck; and, seated on a carpet beside his mistress, he offered her cups.

So they drank joyously, until they were a little drunk; and at length he said:

"O my benefactress, your voice of marvel used to trouble the six theatres. Every time I heard you then, my spirit took wing from me. It is long since you have overcome me in that way. The moon is bright over the shimmering river. The night is deep and solitary. Will you not consent to favor me with a song?"

For a little, Shih-niang refused. Then she looked at the moon, and a song escaped her. It was an affecting melody, taken from one of the pieces of the Yuan dynasty, called "The Light Rose of the Peaches." In truth:

Her voice took flight to the Milky Way,
And the clouds stopped to listen.
Its echo jell into the deep water
and the fishes hastened.

Shih-niang sang. And in a near-by junk there was a young man called Sun; his first name was Fu, Rich, and his surname was Shan-Iai, Excellent-in-Promise. His family was one of the wealthiest in Hsin-an of Hui-chow; his ancestors had owned the salt monopoly in Yang-chow. He was just twenty years old, and had moulded his character in accordance with his passion, being a regular visitor at the blue pavilions, where the smiles of painted roses are to be bought. He was making a journey, and had cast anchor for the night at Kua-chow. He was drinking in solitude, bemoaning the absence of companions.

Suddenly in the night he heard a voice more sweet than the sighs of the bird of passion, or than the warbling phoenix. No words seemed adequate, he felt, to describe the beauty of this song. Walking out from his cabin, he found that the music came from a junk not very far distant from his own.

In his eagerness to know who had enchanted him, he told his men to go and question the boatmen. But he learned no more than that the junk had been hired by Li Chia. He obtained no information concerning the singer. He reflected:

"Such a perfect voice could not belong to a woman of good family. How can I manage to see this bird?"

He could not sleep that night. In the morning, at about the fifth watch, he heard the wind roaring on the water. The light of day was strangely veiled by cloud, and flakes of snow were whirling madly. It has been said:

The clouds are swallowing
Countless thousands of trees upon the hill.
Footprints disappear 'on many footpaths.
The fisher in the bamboo hat
On the frail boat
Catches only snow and the frozen river.

This snowstorm rendered it impossible to cross the river, and the boats could not be set in motion. Sun, therefore, told his rowers to leave his moorings and to make fast alongside Li Chia's junk. Then, in a sable bonnet and wrapped in his fox-skin robe, he opened his cabin window, pretending to look at the white snow as it fell. Shih-niang had just arranged her hair, and, with her tapering fingers, was pushing back the short curtains to throw out the dregs of tea in the bottom of her cup. The freshened splendor of her rouge shone softly.

Sun saw that celestial beauty, that incantation; he scented that perfume; and his soul boiled over. For a long moment he gazed, and his spirit was as if submerged. But he recovered himself and, leaning out of the window, recited, nearly at full voice, the poem of the "Blossom of the Plum Tree":

Snow covers the mountain where the Sage abides,
Under the trees in the moonlight
Beauty advances.

Li Chia heard the poem and came out of his cabin, curious to see who was reciting it. In this way he fell into the trap set by Sun, who hastened to salute him, asking:

"Old-Elder-Brother, what is your honorable name? And what is your first name which one does not presume to repeat?"

Having answered in accordance with the convention, Li Chia had to question Sun in his turn. They exchanged such words as are customary between educated men. Finally the libertine said:

"This snowstorm was sent by Heaven to effect our meeting. It is a large piece of fortune for your little brother. I was lonely and without diversion in my cabin. Would it not be my venerable brother's pleasure that we should go to a riverside pavilion and divert ourselves by drinking wine?"

Li Chia answered:

"The water-chestnuts meet at the caprice of the current. How should I not be glad of this offer?"

"Between the four seas all men are brothers."

Then Sun ordered his servant to come with him, sheltering Li Chia under a large parasol. The two men saluted each other again, landed on the bank and, after walking a little distance, found a wine pavilion.

Having entered, they chose seats by the window and sat down. The attendant brought them hot wine, Sun raised his cup to give the signal, and soon the two were conversing freely and had become friends. At length Sun leaned forward and said in a low voice:

"Last night a song arose from your honorable ship. Whose was that voice?"

Wishing to pose as a man of leisure making a journey, Li Chia at once told the truth:

"It was Tu Shih-niang, the famous singing girl of Peking."

"How comes a singing girl to belong to my brother?"

Li Chia then ingeniously told his story, and the other said:

"To marry such a beauty is exceptional good fortune. But will your honorable father be satisfied?"

Li sighed and answered:

"There is no lack of anxiety in my humble house. My father is of a very stern disposition, and as yet knows nothing."

Sun, developing his hidden traps, continued:

"If your honorable father is not placable, where will my Elder-Brother shelter the Beauty whom he has carried away? Have you come to some arrangement with her on this point?"

With heavy brows, Li answered:

"My little wife and I have already discussed the matter."

"Your Honorable Favor has doubtless some admirable plan?"

"Her idea," explained Li, "is to remain for the time at a place in the country of Su and Hang, whilst I go forward to my family and ask my friends and relations to appease my father."

The other gave a deep sigh and assumed a saddened air:

"Our friendship is not yet deep enough. I fear that you may consider my words both strange and too outspoken."

"When I have the good fortune to receive your learned and enlightening counsel, how could I fail to respect it?"

"Your honorable and noble father, being of stern character, is certainly still angry at your conduct in Peking. And now my Elder-Brother marries in the face of convention. How could your prudent relatives and valuable friends fail to share the views of your honorable father? When you rashly ask them to act on your behalf, they will certainly refuse. Then will not the temporary residence of your Honorable Favor become a permanent one? In your position, it will be as difficult to advance as to retire."

Li Chia knew that he had only fifty ounces in his purse, and that half this sum would very soon have vanished. He could not help hanging his head. His companion added:

"I have yet another thing to say, and it comes from my heart. Will you hear it?"

"Having already received your sympathetic advice, I shall be most happy to listen."

"Since earliest time," said Sun, "the hearts of women have been as changeable as the waves of the sea. And among the Flowers-in-the-Mist especially there are few who are found faithful. Since the present case concerns a famous singing girl, who knows the whole earth, it is probable that she has some former associate in the regions of the South. She has consequently availed herself of your help to conduct her to the land where this other lives."

"I beg to say that that is not certain," protested Li.

"Even if it is not, the men of the South are very adroit and very active. You leave a beautiful woman to live there all alone: can you guarantee that none will climb her wall or penetrate her dwelling? After all, the relations between father and son are from Heaven and cannot be destroyed. If you abandon your family for the sake of a singing girl, you will wander until you become one of those incorrect Floating-on- the-Wave individuals. A woman is not Heaven. You must ponder this matter seriously."

Hearing this, Li Chia felt as if he were swept away by a torrent. At last he answered: "What, in your enlightened opinion, ought I to do?"

"Your servant has a plan which should be very profitable to you. But I fear lest, weakened by the soft pillow of your love, you will not be able to put it into execution, and that my words will therefore be wasted."

"If you have a really good suggestion, I shall be forever your debtor. Why do you fear to speak?"

"My Elder-Brother, for more than a year you have Fluttered-in-the-Rain, obsessed by your brothel. You have not been able to give your mind to the difficulties which will assail you when you no longer know where to sleep or to eat. Your father's anger is only due to your having become infatuated with Flowers, besotted by Willows, until you poured out gold as if it were simple sand. He tells himself that you will quickly consume the abundant wealth of your family, and not be assured of having children. By returning empty-handed you will justify his anger. If, O my Elder-Brother, you could cut the knot which binds you to your love, I would willingly make you a gift of a thousand ounces. With a thousand ounces of silver to show your father, you could say that, during your stay at the capital, you had rarely left your study chamber and that you had never Skimmed the Waves. He will have confidence in you, and the harmony of the house will be restored. Thus, without idle words, you change your sorrow to joy. Give the matter three thoughts. I do not covet the Beauty! I speak with no idea but of loyally helping a friend."

Li Chia was a man of naturally weak character; moreover, he was afraid of his father. Sun's fine words troubled his heart. He rose, made a deep bow, and said:

"O Brother! Your noble counsel has cleared away the foolish and tangled obstruction of my understanding. But my little favorite has accompanied me for some thousands of li, and it would not be just for me to leave her in this way. I will return to deliberate with her, and to discover whether her mind is favorable to your project. 1 shall inform you shortly."

"In our conversation," answered Sun, "we have abandoned the paths of strict politeness.

"That was because my loyal heart could not endure to see the separation of a father and son, and wished to help you to return to your family."

They both drank another cup of wine. The wind had dropped, and the snow had ceased to fall. The color of the sky proclaimed the evening. Sun caused his servant to pay for the drinks, and, taking Li Chia by the hand, accompanied him as far as the junk. It is very true that:

You meet a stranger and say three words
And tear off a piece of your heart.

In the morning Shih-niang, on being left alone in her cabin, had prepared a little feast for her friend, wishing to spend the day with him in happiness; but the sun had set before Chia came back. She had lanterns lit to guide him and, when he at last appeared and entered the cabin, raised her eyes to his face and found the color of displeasure. She poured out a cup of hot wine and offered it to him; but he shook his head without a word, and refused to drink. Then he went and threw himself on the bed. Sad at heart, Shih-niang put the cups and dishes in order. She then undid her husband's clothes and, leaning on the pillow, gently asked him:

"What news have you heard that has so upset you?"

Li Chia sighed, but without answering. She questioned him again three or four times, but he was already asleep. Unable to be indifferent to such lack of regard, she remained for a long time sitting on the edge of the bed, incapable of sleep.

In the middle of the night he awoke and gave another deep sigh; and she said to him:

"What is this difficult matter with which my Lord is troubled? What are these sighings?"

Li Chia threw off the blanket and seemed about to speak, but the words would not come from him. His lips trembled like leaves, and finally he burst out sobbing. She clasped his head with one arm and held it against her breast, trying to comfort him, and saying tenderly:

"The love which unites us has lasted for many days, for very nearly two years. We have overcome a thousand hardships and bitter moments, but now we are far beyond all difficulty. Why do you show such grief to-day, when we are about to cross the river and to taste the joy of a hundred years? There must surely be a reason. All things are shared in common between husband and wife, in life and after death. If anything is the matter, we must discuss it. Why do you hide your sorrow from me?" Thus urged, the young man mastered his tears and said: "I am crushed beneath the woe which Heaven heaps upon me. In the generosity of your soul, you have not cast me by. You have endured a thousand wrongs for me. That is no merit of mine. But I still think of my father, whose commands I am defying and that against every convention and all laws. He is of inflexible character, and I fear that his wrath will grow double at the sight of me. Where, then, shall we two, floating with the current, come to our anchorage?

How shall I ensure our happiness, when my father has broken with me? To-day my friend Sun invited me to drink and spoke to me of my prospects, and what he said has pierced my heart."

"What is my Lord's intention?" she asked in great surprise.

"I was turning madly in the web of our affairs, when my friend Sun sketched out an excellent plan to me. But I fear that my benefactress will refuse to allow it."

"Who is this friend, Sun? If his plan is good, why should I not agree to it?"

"His first name is Fu, and his family had the salt monopoly at Hsin-an. He is a man who has Drifted-in-the-Wind and knows life. Last night he was charmed by your pure song. I told him where we came from, and confided the difficulties which beset our return. Then, under the impulsion of a generous thought, he offered to give me a thousand ounces if you will marry him. With these thousand ounces as testimony I shall be able to speak to my father. Also I shall know that you are not without shelter. But I cannot contain my feeling, and that is why I mourn."

And his tears fell like a storm of rain. Ceasing to hold his head against her breast, Shih-niang gently pushed him aside. At last she smiled like ice and said to him:

"This person must be a hero, a man of courage and virtue, to have conceived a project so advantageous to my Lord. Not only will my Lord have a thousand ounces to take back with him, not only will your slave gain shelter, but your baggage will be lighter also and more easily handled. As a plan it satisfies both convention and convenience. Where are the thousand ounces?"

Struggling with his tears, Li Chia replied:

"I have not got your consent, so the silver was not given me.

"You must demand it first thing to-morrow morning. A thousand ounces is a considerable sum, and it must all be paid into your hand before I enter his cabin. For I am not merchandise which may be bought on credit."

It was then the fourth watch of the night.

Shih-niang prepared her toilet-table, saying: "To-day I must adorn myself to bid farewell to my former protector and to do honor to my new one. It is no commonplace event. I must therefore take great pains with paint and perfume, and put on my best jewels and embroidered robes."

Thereafter, with perfume and paint and jewelry, she added to the splendor of her petalled seduction. The sun had already risen before she completed her preparations.

Li Chia was disturbed, and yet seemed almost happy. Shih-niang urged him to insist upon the payment of the money, and he at once carried her answer to the other junk. Then Sun said:

"It is easy for me to give the money; but I ought to have the fair one's jewelry as a proof of her consent."

Li Chia told this to Shih-niang, who pointed to the casket with the golden lock, and caused it to be taken to

Sun, who joyfully counted out a thousand ounces of silver and sent them to Li's ship. The young woman herself verified the weight and standard of the metal; and then, leaning over the bulwarks, half opened her scarlet lips and showed her white teeth, saying to the dazzled Sun:

"You can now, I think, give me back my casket for a time. The Lord Li's passports are in it, and I must return them to him."

The other at once ordered the little chest to be brought back and placed on the bridge. Shih-niang opened it. Inside there were several compartments, and she asked Li Chia to help her lift out each in turn.

In the first there were jewels in the shape of king-fisher feathers, jasper pins, and precious earrings, to the value of many hundred ounces. Shih-niang took up these things in handfuls and threw them into the river. Li, Sun and the boatmen uttered exclamations of dismay.

In the second compartment were a jade flute and a golden flageolet. In a third were antique jewels, gold furnishings and a hundred ornaments worth thousands of ounces each. She threw them all into the river. The stricken onlookers gave voice to their regret.

Finally she drew out a box filled with pearls and rubies and emeralds and cats' eyes, whose number and value were beyond computation. The cries of the wondering bystanders beat in the air like thunder. She wanted to throw all these into the river also; but Li Chia held her in his arms, while Sun vehemently encouraged him.

So, pushing Li away, she turned to the other and reviled him:

"The Lord Li and I suffered many bitter moments before we came to yesterday. And you, to serve a detestable and criminal lust, have undone us and have caused me to hate the man I loved. After my death I meet the Spirit of Retribution, and I shall not forget your vile hypocrisy."

Then, turning toward Li Chia, she continued:

"During those many years when I lived in a disorder of the dust and breeze, I secretly amassed these treasures, that they might some day rescue my body. When I met my Lord, we vowed that our union should be higher than the mountain, deeper than the sea. We swore that, even when our hair was white, we should have our love. Before leaving the capital, I pretended to receive this casket as a gift from my friends. It contained a treasure of more than a myriad ounces. I intended to deposit it in your treasury, when I had seen your father and mother. Who would have thought your faith so shallow, that, on the strength of a chance conversation, you would consent to lose my loyal heart? To-day, before the eyes of all these people, I have shown you that your thousand ounces were a very little sum of money. These persons are my witness that it is my Lord who rejects his wife, that it is not 1 who am wanting in my duty."

Hearing these sad words, those who were present wept, and called down curses upon Li, and reviled him as an ingrate. And he, being both ashamed and desolate, shed tears of bitter repentance. He knelt down to beg for her forgiveness. But Shih-niang, holding the jewels in each hand, leaped into the yellow water of the river.

The onlookers uttered a cry and rushed to save her. But, under a sombre cloud, the waves in the heart of the river broke into boiling foam, and no further trace was seen of that desperate woman.

Alas! she was an illustrious singing girl, as beautiful as flowers or jade. She had been swallowed in an instant by the water.

The people, grinding their teeth, would have beaten Li and Sun; but these, in terror and dismay, made haste to push their boats out from the bank, and then went each his own way.

Li Chia, seeing the thousand ounces of silver in his cabin, unceasingly wept for the death of Shih-niang. His remorse gave birth to a kind of madness in him, of which he could never be healed.

Sun was so prostrated that he had to keep his bed. He thought he saw Shih-niang standing in front of him all day and every day. It was not long before he expiated his crime in death.

We must now tell how Liu, having left the capital to return to his own village, also halted at Kua-chow. Leaning over the river to take up some water in a bronze basin, he let the thing slip, and therefore begged certain fishermen to drag their net for it.

When they drew up, there was a little box in the net. Liu opened it, and it was full of pearls and precious stones. He rewarded the fishermen generously, and placed the box near his pillow.

In the night he had a dream. A young woman rose from the troubled waters of the river, and he recognized Shih-niang. She drew near, wishing him ten thousand happinesses. Then she recounted the unworthy ingratitude of Li, and said: "Of your bounty you gave me a hundred and fifty ounces. I have not forgotten your generosity, and I put this little box in the fishermen's net as an offering of recognition."

He awoke and, having learned thus of Shih-niang's death, sighed for a long time.

Later, those who told me this story declared that Sun, since he thought he could acquire a beautiful woman for a thousand ounces, was evidently not a respectable man. Li Chia, they said, had not understood the sorrowful heart of Shih-niang, and was consequently stupid, without refinement, and not worthy of mention. Shih-niang alone was heroic. She was, in fact, unique since furthest antiquity. Why could she not meet some charming companion, some phoenix worthy of her? Why did she make the mistake of loving Li Chia? An admirable piece of jade was thrown to him who did not deserve it; so that love turned to hate, and a thousand passionate impulses were drowned in the deep water. Alas!

Tu Shih-niang nu ch'en pai pao hsiang. (Tu Shih-niang, being put to shame drowns herself with her casket of a hundred treasures.) Chin ku chi'i kuan (17th Century.)

THE WEDDING OF YA-NEI

In the reign of the Emperor Shen Tsung there lived an official named Wu, who was at that time Governor of Ch'ang-sha. His wife, Lin, had given him a son named Ya-nei, or "In-the- Palace," who had that year reached the age of sixteen. He was well endowed, although not without tendency to wantonness; yet he had from childhood diligently studied the classics and poetry. He had only one really extravagant failing; to satisfy his appetite he needed: more than three bushels of rice every day, and over two pounds of meat. We will say nothing of his drinking. In spite of all this, he ever seemed half starved.

About the third Moon of that year, Wu was appointed Governor of Yang-chow, and the equipages and boats of his new post came up to meet him. He packed his belongings, said good-bye to his friends and went on board, following the course of the river. On the second day he had to stop, because of a storm of wind which raised up the waters of the river in great waves.

At the point on the fiver bank where the boat lay moored, there was already another official junk, before the cabin of which stood a middle-aged matron and a charming girl, surrounded by several women slaves. Ya-nei perceived the youthful beauty, and thought her so seductive that he immediately composed the following poem:

Her soul has the tenderness of Autumn rivers
And her pure bones are made of jade.
The rose of the hibiscus lightens her,
Her eyebrows have the curve of willow leaves.
Is she not an Immortal from the Jasper Lake
Or from the Moon Palace?

He looked at her so ardently that his troubled soul took flight and alighted upon the maiden's breast. But his intelligence at once conceived a plan, and he said to his father:

"Tieh-tieh, why would you not tell the sailors to anchor our junk by the side of that one? Would it not be safer?"

Wu was also of this opinion and accordingly gave orders to his men. When the vessel was alongside, he sent to inquire the name of the voyagers, and was informed that they were a certain Ho Chang, the new Governor of Kien-K'ang, going to his post with his wife Ho Tsin, and his daughter Elegant, who was just fifteen.

Wu had known the excellent man formerly, so he had his name carried to him. Then, clothed in his official robes, he stepped from one ship to the other. His colleague was awaiting him before his cabin, and, having exchanged formal greetings, they sat and talked together, drinking a cup of tea. Wu returned to his boat where, after a few moments, Ho Chang returned his visit. And Ya-nei was present at the meeting. Ho Chang had no son, and took pleasure in seeing this beautiful young man. He questioned him upon certain ancient and modern books, and was satisfied with the ready answers which he obtained. He praised him unreservedly for them, thinking:

"This is just the son-in-law that I should like. He would make an unprecedented match with my daughter. But he is going to live at Pien-liang, and I will be at Kien-K'ang which is more than fifteen days' journey to the south of that place."

Wu asked him:

"How many sons have you, O Old-Man-Born-Before-Me?"

"I will hot conceal from you the fact that I have only a daughter,"

Wu considered:

"That charming child was his daughter then. She would be an unprecedented wife for my son. But she is his only child, and he certainly would not be willing to marry her at any great distance from himself."

He added aloud:

"But if you have no son, you have only to take concubines."

"I thank you for your suggestion. It had occurred to me."

After having talked for some time, Ho Chang withdrew to his cabin, where his wife and daughter were awaiting him. Being a little elated by his cups of wine, he kept speaking of Ya-nei's merit, and of his intention to invite the father and son for the next day. His words sank deeply into his daughter's mind.

On the following day the river was still churned by waves, and the storm sent up spray to a height of more than thirty feet. The crash of water was heard on all sides.

Early in the morning Ho Chang sent his invitation, and, when the two men arrived, the feast began. Elegant, in the next cabin, could see Ya-nei through the cracks in the bulkhead, and her heart was secretly moved.

"If I could have him for my husband, my desire would be satisfied. But I shall not persuade him into a proposal by merely looking at him. How shall I set about making known my thought of him?"

Ya-nei, for his part, looked in vain for some means of speaking to his neighbor. When the meal was finished, he returned to his ship and lay down on his bed.

But Elegant was so much occupied in thinking of the young man that she could not touch her dinner. Leaving her mother alone, she retired to rest and was on the point of 1
going to sleep, when the sound of a song came to her. It was the voice of Ya-nei, singing:

A dream has come to me from the Blue Bowl,
But I was not able to speak.
I could not tell her of my delight
Or appoint an endless alliance.

She rose softly, opened her cabin door without sound and went up on to the bridge. Ya-nei was standing on the other ship, and immediately leaped to her side, and boldly took her in his arms. Between joy and alarm, she did not dare to resist. He drew her into her cabin and loosened her garments.

At that moment one of the slaves passed before the cabin and, seeing the door open, cried out:

"The door is open! O thieves!"

Elegant at once covered her lover with the blanket, but one of the slaves saw the invader's feet. Ho Chang and his wife snatched away the blanket.

"How does this wretch dare to dishonor my family?" cried the Governor in a rage. "Ah, throw him into the river!"

In spite of the prayers of the culprit and the girl two men seized the former, dragged him away and threw him into the water. She followed him in despair, crying:

"I have ruined him! I wish to follow!"

And she too threw herself into the water. She woke with a start. It was only a dream.

Till morning she lay and thought, wondering if this dream were perhaps an omen that her destiny ought not to be bound up with that of Ya-nei.

He also had complicated dreams that night. He rose in the morning and opened the port-hole of his cabin. Ho Chang's ship was touching his own, and the port-hole opposite to him was open. Elegant appeared there, and their eyes met. Surprised, delighted and embarrassed, they smiled, as if they had known each other for a long time. They would gladly have spoken, but were afraid of being heard. Then she made a small sign to him, retired quickly into her cabin, and rapidly wrote some words on a piece of paper ornamented with sprays of rose peach. She rolled it in a silk handkerchief and cleverly threw it to Ya-nei, who caught it in both hands. They saluted each other, and reclosed their port-holes.

He unfolded the handkerchief and smoothed out the crinkled leaf. It bore this poem:

Brocade characters are on this paper of flowers,
And the bowels of my sorris in this embroidery.
I have dreamed of a prince
And, carried upon a cloud, I come to him.

But there was also a little word or two added:

"This evening your submissive mistress will await you near the lamp. The noise of my scissors will be the signal for our happiness, and of our meeting."

Beyond himself with joy, the lad hastened to take a leaf of golden paper and wrote out a poem on it. Then he took off his embroidered silken girdle, rolled it all together, and opened his port-hole. Elegant had also opened hers; she received the small packet and at once concealed it in her sleeve, for she heard the slaves approaching. These were followed by her mother. At last the time came for her father to cross to the other ship for the return feast given by Wu.

Full of cunning, the maiden took a vessel brimming with liquor and gave it to her slaves, who eyed the gift as a thirsty dragon looks upon water. They were half-drunk when Ho Chang came back from the feast, and Elegant told them to go to bed, and that she would do some needle-work. As their faces were red, their ears burning and their legs unsteady, they were only too glad to retire; and soon their snores were heard over the ship. Little by little all other sounds died away in both the junks. Then she gently knocked on her port-hole with her scissors.

Naturally Ya-nei was waiting for the signal; as soon as he heard it, his body was as if it had been shaken to pieces. However, he softly opened his shutter, stepped from one ship to the other, and glided into the cabin where the maiden awaited him. She gave him formal greeting, which he returned; but they lookied at each other under the lamp, and their passion already raged like fire. They could hardly exchange a word, and Ya-nei's trembling hands were undoing her garments. She offered a feeble resistance. He carried her on to the bed, and with his arms joined himself to the fresh breast that lighted him.

At last they were able to speak. She told him of her dream, and of her astonishment on recognizing, in his poem, the verses which she had heard him sing in dream. He turned pale and sat down:

"My dream was exactly yours. Before these omens are fulfilled, I shall speak to my father to arrange our marriage."

But, even as they talked, they silently fell asleep in each other's arms.

Now about the middle of the night, the wind fell and the river became calmer. At the fifth watch the sailors untied their moorings and began to haul their anchors, singing at their work. The noise awakened the lovers, who heard the men say:

"The ship catches the wind rarely. We shall not be long in getting to Ch'i-Chow."

They looked at each other in dismay:

"What are we going to do now?"

"Hush!" said she. "You must remain hidden for the moment. We will at last find a plan."

"It is our dream come true."

Remembering that the slaves had seen her lover's feet in her dream, Elegant leaned forward and covered them carefully with an ample blanket. At last she said:

"I have a plan. During the day you must hide under the couch, and I shall pretend to be ill, and keep in bed, or in the cabin. When we reach Ch'i-Chow, I will give you a little money, and you must escape in the confusion of the disembarkation. You shall rejoin your parents, and we will arrange for our marriage. If, by any chance, my parents were to refuse, we should tell the truth. My family has always loved me excessively; they will certainly accede."

As soon as they had determined on their course, Ya-nei slid under the bed, and made himself a place among the baggages. The curtain fell into place in front of him, and the young girl was still in bed when her mother came in, saying:

"Aya! Why are you resting like this?"

"I do not feel very well. I must have taken cold."

"Cover yourself well, my daughter, if that be so."

At this moment a slave entered, asking if she should bring breakfast.

"My child," said her mother, "if you are not well, you would do better not to take any solid nourishment. I am going to make you an occasional small rice broth until you are recovered."

"I am not very fond of broth. Give me some rice. Let them bring it to me here. I shall eat it by and by."

"I will keep you company."

"Aya! If you do not go and look after this rabble of women, they will do their work most incontestable wrong."

Without understanding, the mother did indeed go to the next cabin at that moment when the breakfast was brought in. As soon as she had turned her back, Elegant told the slave to set down the dish on the table.

"You may go away. I shall call you when I have finished."

Ya-nei was watching, and came out from his hiding. On the dish there were only two small bowls of vegetables mixed with meat, a bowl of cooked green-stuff, and a little rice. Naturally, the young girl was not in the habit of taking large quantities of food; but for her lover, with his three bushels of rice a day, the matter was otherwise. After their meal, he again glided under the bed, nearly as hungry as before. She called the slave, and told her to bring in two more bowls of rice.

Her mother heard this, and entered, saying:

"My child! You are not well. How is it that you want to eat all that?"

"The reason is not far to seek," she answered. "I am hungry, that is all."

And her father, who had come to see the invalid, said:

"Let her be. She is growing, and needs nourishment."

When night came, and the evening meal was finished, she shut the door and told her lover he could get into the bed again. But the poor young man was suffering cruelly from hunger.

"Our stratagem," said he, "is admirable. But it is in one respect also grievous. I cannot conceal from you that my appetite is considerable. The three meals which I have had to-day seem scarcely a mouthful. On such a diet, I shall starve before we come to Ch'i-Chow."

"Why did you not say so? I shall make them bring me more to-morrow."

"But are you not afraid of rousing suspicion?"

"That is nothing. I shall see to it. But how much would you need?"

"We shall never be able to obtain quite that. Ten bowls of rice at each meal would not be enough."

Next day, when her parents came to see her, Elegant complained.

"I do not know what is the matter with me," she said. "I am dying of hunger."

But her mother began to laugh:

"That is not a very serious affair. I will have more rice brought to you."

But when the young girl said that she needed about ten bowls, the good woman was startled. She again wished to remain near her daughter.

"If you stay here, mama, I shall not be able to take anything. Leave me alone, and I shall eat more comfortably."

Everybody indulged her caprice. When the cabin was empty, she shut the door and Ya-nei came out. Hungry as he was, he made the ten bowls vanish like a shooting star, and did not leave a single grain. Elegant watched him with astonishment, and asked him in a low voice:

"Is that still too little?"

"It will suffice," answered the other, drinking a cup of tea.

He hastened back to his hiding-place, while the young girl ate some vegetables. Then she called the slaves, who came running up, wondering whether she had been able to eat all that food. They looked at the empty bowls and at their mistress's slim figure, and murmured as they went away:

"What a terrible illness!"

One of them, in her anxiety, went to the father and showed him the dish, suggesting that he should call a doctor as soon as possible. And he, for his part, forbade them to give her so much another time, fearing that she would burst.

At mid-day he went himself to speak to her.

She began to weep: her mother took her part; and they gave way to her. The evening meal was just as large.

They were approaching Ch'i-Chow, and Ho Chang, who was really alarmed, ordered his boatmen to cast anchor near the town. Early in the morning he sent his steward to find the best doctor, and when the man arrived, brought him on board and explained the case to him. They then went to examine the invalid and to try her pulse. The doctor at length came back with the father into the central cabin.

"Well? What is the illness?"

The other coughed, and at last said:

"Your daughter is suffering-from lack of nourishment."

Her father was staggered:

"But I have told you that she ate thirty bowls of rice yesterday."

"Yet, but your daughter is still a child. She is apparently fifteen years old, but that is equivalent to fourteen in reality, or even to thirteen and some months. Her food accumulates in her stomach, but is not assimilated. From this cause arises the fever which burns her stomach and makes her imagine herself to be always hungry. The more she eats, therefore, the more her stomach burns. In one month it will be too late to cure her, and she will die of hunger."

"But how is she to be cured?"

"First, I shall make her digest what she eats. Of course, she must eat very little indeed."

He wrote his prescription and went away. The servant went to get the drugs, which were dissolved and boiled according to direction, and finally presented to the young girl.

She said that she would take them, and as soon as she was alone threw them out of the port-hole. Thereafter she continued to ask for ten bowls of rice for every meal.

Everyone on the ship was now discussing this extraordinary case. Some said that they ought to call in sorcerers. Others thought that religious men would do better, seeing that she had certainly been possessed by one of those starving spirits which wander without purpose in punishment for their sins, with a needle's eye for a mouth, seeking in vain for food.

At the next town, Ho Chang summoned another doctor. After his examination, mention was made of the former diagnosis, and he burst out laughing.

"Nothing of the sort. It is an internal consumption."

"But what, then, is the reason for this hunger?"

"The hot and the cold principles are at variance m her, and the resultant fire gives her continual opsomania. It is easy to understand."

"But she has no fever."

"Outside she is cool, but she burns within. The malady is inside the bones; and that is why it is not visible. If she had continued to take the drugs which you have been giving her, it would have been difficult to save her. I shall give her something to soothe her bowels. She will then, of her own accord, refuse all food."

It need not be said that it was the same in this case as in the other. All the medicines went down the river.

Meanwhile the two lovers continued to profit by the silence of the night. Naturally, the young girl was at first, so to speak, passive in the arms of the young man, who was himself bashful. But little by little, penetrating further into the domain of pleasure, their amorous intelligence redoubled with their rapture, and they forgot entirely where they were.

One night a slave woke up, and heard a "tsi-tsi-nung-nung" and a "tsia-tsia" coming from the bed, and then quick breathing. Inwardly surprised, she next day told her mistress, and the mother, seeing that her daughter was always of a brilliantly healthy complexion, began to think this unknown- malady a very strange one. She did not inform her husband, however, but ran herself to see her daughter. The child's face seemed to her to be more beautiful and animated even than usual. She went out, without seeing anything which might confirm her suspicion, and, coming back again after breakfast, began gently to question her daughter on her ideas of marriage.

As they were talking, there suddenly came a snore from under the bed. Ya-nei, after his efforts in the night and his morning meal, had gone to sleep in his hiding-place.

Elegant's mother at once shut the door and, quickly stooping to look under the bed, saw the young man asleep.

"Alas, how could you do this thing? And then frighten us with your illness? Now everybody will know of it. Where does he come from? May Heaven strike him dead!"

Elegant's face was purple with shame.

"It is all your child's fault. He is the son of the Lord Wu."

"Ya-nei? But you have never seen him! Besides, he was at the dinner with your father, and we came away at midnight. How can he be here?"

Trusting in her mother's indulgence, the young girl confessed everything, and added:

"Your unworthy daughter has dishonored our name and lost her innocence. My crime is unpardonable. But it was the will of Heaven. There had to be that storm to make us meet, and then destiny prevented our betrothal. Our strength was too small for the struggle, and we have sworn to love each other until death. I implore you to speak to my father and appease him; for if he makes an uproar; there is nothing left for me but to die."

Her tears fell like rain. And, while they were talking, Ya- nei's snores sounded like thunder.

"At least make him keep quiet," cried the mother in a fury. "We can no longer hear ourselves speak."

And she went out, slamming the door, while Elegant hastened to awaken the sleeper.

"Really you might snore less loudly!" she said with impatience. "All is discovered now."

When he heard this, Ya-nei's body was frozen with terror as if he had received a drenching in cold water. His teeth chattered.

"Do not be afraid. I have asked my mother to speak for us. If my father is angry, there will be time enough for us to die then."

The woman meanwhile had hurried to her husband, but there was a slave with him, putting the cabin in order. So she waited, and the tears rolled from her eyes. Ho Chang thought she was anxous about her daughters' health, and reassured her:

"She will be better in a few days. The doctor said so. Do not disturb yourself."

But she sneered at him:

"You have been listening to the flower words of old Wise-Wand. Better in a few days! She would have to be ill first!"

"What do you mean?"

Since the servant was no longer there, she told him in a low voice what she had seen and heard. Ho Chang's anger was such that his sight was troubled. She begged him to calm himself.

"Enough! Enough!" he thundered. "This worthless daughter fouls the very air upon our threshold. We must kill them both in the night, so that none may know."

The woman's face became as the earth.

"We have already reached a ripe age, and this is the only flesh and bone we have. If you kill her, what will be left to us? As for Ya-nei, he is of a good family, he is intelligent, and well-built. Our stations are identical and our houses equal. His only fault is that he did not make a proposal, but rather forced everything in secret. Yet so the matter is. Would it not be better to send him back with a letter to Wu, requiring gifts of betrothal? We would lose all by making a scandal."

Ho Chang's rage was already half spent, and he now let himself be persuaded by degrees. He went out and asked the boatmen where they were.

"We are approaching Wu-ch'ang."

"You will anchor there."

He then called his confidential steward and, explaining all to him, gave him a letter. After this he went to see his daughter, who hid herself under the blanket when she beheld him. He spoke no word to her; but in a stern tone called out Ya-nei, who crept from his hiding-place, saluted the older man, and said:

"My crime deserves death."

"How could a young man of your education commit such an act? My wife has prevailed upon me to spare your life; but, if you would redeem your fault, you must take my unworthy daughter as your wife. If this is not your intention, do not count upon my pardon."

Ya-nei abased himself in ritual prostration.

"The honor which you do me is a reward which my conduct does not deserve," he said. "I shall speak to my parents as soon as I return."

Ho Chang hurried him away, without leaving him time to speak to the young girl again. She was clinging to her mother, and whispered:

"I do not know my father's intention. Could I not have a letter from Ya-nei on his arrival?"

Her truly indulgent mother went and spoke to the steward.

The latter had already hired a boat, and, as it was night, the intruder would be able to pass from one junk to the other without being observed. They set out, while Elegant wept incessantly for sorrow and uneasiness. We must now return to the family of Wu.

After the night of Ya-nei's departure, their boat had proceeded for several leagues before the young man's absence was noticed. But when they called for him, and his cabin was found empty, the souls of his parents left their bodies. They howled their despair, supposing that their child had fallen unobserved into the water.

They turned the ship about, hoping at least to recover the body; but all searching was in vain, and they had perforce to resume their journey in despair.

They had been at their destination for two days when Ya-nei arrived; you may suppose that their surprise was only equalled by their joy. They read Ho Chang's letter, and understood everything. They scolded their son, and made a feast for Ho Chang's envoy. When the betrothal gifts were ready, they sent them in charge of their steward, to whom Ya-nei entrusted a secret letter for his Elegant.

Soon the time came for Ya-nei's examination at the capital, and he was accepted. His father asked for a holiday, and the whole family went to Kien-K'ang, where the marriage was celebrated. The fame of Elegant's wisdom and beauty grew with the years, and the happiness of these two was never dimmed.

Hsing shih heng yen (1627),
28th Tale.

A STRANGE DESTINY

In epochs of deep peace
When days are lengthening,
The flute sounds and songs are heard
Among the drunken villages.
The Phoenix Car is said to be approaching
With the Emperor,
And each one turns his eye
To the splendor of that procession.

In the reign of Hui Tsung of the Sung dynasty, near the capital of the East, on the borders of the Lake of Clearness of Gold, a new wine pavilion had just been opened, under the sign of The Quick Hedge. Fan, the landlord, and his brother, Erh-lang, were the proprietors. Neither of them was married; and their business prospered.

It was the week when Spring melts into Summer, and men walk abroad in number to enjoy the freshness and beauty of nature.

One day Erh-lang roamed the lake-side, delighting in the soft air, and saw, in front of a tea-house, a ravishing girl of about eighteen, in whose face, which was as dreamful as the Night Star, flowered all the blossoms of the time. He stopped, fixed to the ground with admiration and already riotous with love. He could not take his eyes from the rose radiance of this face, peach blossom against flawless jade; from this slender body, from the rare golden lotus of these delicate feet. A scarlet hibiscus in flower framed this phoenix against the stirring landscape of the great lake.

Alas! our emotions do not depend upon our will. The young girl felt herself looked upon, and raised her eyes; her soul was at once troubled, her child's heart secretly rejoiced. She thought:

"If I could marry this beautiful man, I should know many happy moments. But, though he is there now, where will he be to-morrow? How can I tell him how to find me again?"

Just then a seller of refreshments came by with his small vessels on his shoulder. She called him:

"Have you a little honey-water?"

The merchant set down a bronze vase on the ground to serve her; but she, with pretended clumsiness, upset the vase, and said to him: "Never mind! Come to my house and I will pay for all. I will give you my name and address."

Erh-lang pricked his ears, as she continued: "I am the daughter of Lord Chou, who lives near the Ts'ao Gate. My little name is Victorious-Immortal. And I pray you do not charge too much, for I am not yet betrothed or married."

The young lover trembled with joy, saying to himself:

"These words are meant for me, I am sure of that."

The merchant was meanwhile protesting, and the young girl added:

"My father is not at home just now. But he is terrible, and you will undoubtedly be prosecuted if you try to rob us."

Erh-lang earnestly desired to make himself known in his turn, and being unable to think of any other expedient, he did as the girl had done: asked for a bowl of cool water, and pretended clumsily to upset the full jar. He then said: "Aya! Here is another misfortune! But it does not matter.

Come to my house, and you shall be well recompensed. I am Erh-lang, brother of Fan. We are proprietors of THE PAVILION OF THE QUICK HEDGE. I am nineteen, and no one has yet cheated me in my business, I can draw a bow, and am not yet betrothed."

"Are you not a little mad?" asked the merchant, looking at him in astonishment. "Why do you tell me all that? Do you wish me to act as the go-between for your marriage? I am an honest man, and have never cheated anybody."

Hearing her admirer's words, the girl rejoiced in her heart. She suggested to her mother, who was sitting by her, that they should go away; and rising to her feet, said to the merchant: "If you will follow us, we will pay you at once."

But her eyes spoke in reality to the young man; who walked slowly behind her, admiring the poise of her gait. In this manner they proceeded until the two women entered their house. But the young girl came back almost at once to draw aside the big door-curtain and to look out at him as he passed. He went on walking to and fro, as if he had lost his senses, and did not return to his house till evening.

From that particular day Victorious-Immortal remained so strangely affected that she was quite unable to swallow a. grain of rice, or even to touch a cake. At last, one morning, she was too weak to rise. Her mother ran to her bed.

"My poor child," she asked, "what is the matter with you?"

"I ache all over my body. I have pains in my head and cough a little."

Her mother at once thought of calling in a doctor; but, in the absence of the master of the house and his servant, there was no man to go on the errand. But an old female attendant, named Kind-Welcome, was present and observed:

"The ancient woman Wang lives, as you know, quite close at hand. She has helped more than a hundred children into the world. She can sew, and she can act as go-between; but she can also feel a pulse and diagnose an illness. Everybody calls her as soon as there is anything the matter."

"That is true. Go and fetch her quickly."

Some few moments later the healer came and the mother began a long explanation. But the woman interrupted her:

"I shall know all about it when I have examined the patient."

The sick girl put out a wasted hand, and the woman felt her pulse for a long time. At last she said:

"You have pains in the head, and all your body aches. You are in continual agony, and the earth is hateful to you."

"That is exactly the case," she answered from her bed. "Also I cough a little."

"But what has caused this illness?"

As the girl did not answer, this wise old visitor turned to the mother and the attendant, and signed them to go away. They dared not refuse, and left the room.

"Now we are going to cure you. The illness lies in your heart, and nowhere else."

"In my heart?" questioned the sick girl. "You have seen a handsome young man, and he pleases you. Your suffering rises from that; is it not so?"

"There is nothing of the sort," denied the other.

"Come, come! Tell me the truth, and I will soon find a means to save your life."

Seeing a chance to reach to her desire, little Victorious-Immortal decided to tell everything. When she had finished, the very old woman said:

"Do not be troubled. I know one of his relations who has spoken to me of him. He is intelligent and level-headed.

I shall go and see his brother, to make arrangements for your marriage, if you finally wish to marry him."

"You know very well that I do," said the sick child with a smile. "But will my mother consent?" "Do not be uneasy. I have my methods." She was already out of the room, and saying to the mother: "I know what is the matter with your daughter. If you would like me to make it clear to you, have two cups of wine brought in."

Kind-Welcome made haste to arrange all on the table. The healer drank a draught of burning wine and, turning to the mother, repeated word for word what the girl had confessed to her, adding:

"And now there is nothing for it but to marry her to Erh-lang, for otherwise her death is certain."

"My husband will be away for a long time yet. I cannot decide without him."

"You have only to make the arrangements. You need not celebrate the marriage until after my Lord's return. She must be given her desire; there is no other way of saving her."

"If the young man is as desirable as all that…" the mother murmured uneasily. "But how shall we bring the thing about?"

"I am going to speak to his elder brother. I will keep you informed."

Without further delay, the venerable go-between went straight to The Pavilion of the Quick Hedge, where she found Fan behind his counter, and saluted him:

"Ten thousand happinesses!"

"You come at the right time," he answered with a bow. "I was about to send to beg you to do so. For some days, I assure you, my brother has not been able to take a morsel of food. He says that his whole body is aching, and now he stays in bed. Will you, please, feel his pulse?"

"I will see him. But it is better for me to be alone with him."

"Then I shall not come with you."

So the old woman went up into the sick man's room, and he said to her feebly:

"Mother Wang, it is very long since I saw you. Alas! You come too late! My life is finished!"

"In what special way are you so seriously ill?" she asked, sitting near the bed and touching his wrist.

After a moment she continued:

"Shall I tell you the name of your illness? It is called Vietoriousr-Immortal, little daughter of Chou, and her house is near the Ts'ao Gate."

The sick man was startled and sat up:

"How do you know that?"

"Her family has commissioned me to come and arrange your marriage."

Immediate happiness revived the young man.

He rose and came down with the wise visitor to his astonished brother.

"I am cured," he announced. "And all goes very well."

Meanwhile the old woman was saying: "The family of Chou has sent me especially to talk to you about a marriage."

All was soon settled, the first gifts were exchanged, and the comforted hearts of the two young people were filled with joy. But they had to wait Lord Chou's return before proceeding with the ceremony.

Chou did not come back until eight months later. It is needless to say that, when he did so, all his relations and friends came to drink cups of wine with him to "wash down the dust of the journey." At last his wife told him what had happened, affirming that all was decided. But the eyes of the master of the house became round and white, and he bellowed:

"O filthy imbecile, who gave you the right to betroth our daughter to a wine merchant? Is there no son of decent family who would marry her? Do you wish to make us a laughingstock?"

While he was thus cursing his wife, the servant came up to them, crying:

"Come quickly and save the child! She was behind the door, and heard your cries. She fell down and is no longer breathing."

Stumbling in her haste, the mother ran out. She saw her daughter lying on the ground and was about to raise her, but her husband prevented her, saying:

"Leave her! She was bringing dishonor on us! If she is to die, then let her die!"

Seeing her mistress held back, Kind-Welcome bent over the girl. But Chou, with a blow that made the air whistle between his fingers, sent her against the wall. In his rage, he seized his wife and shook her roughly, and she howled like a dog. The neighbors heard her and ran in, fearing that there was disaster. Soon the room was filled with women, all talking at the same time. But the master of it roughly bade them be silent:

"I do not allow any spying upon my private affairs."

The neighbors retired in discomfort, and the mother threw herself upon her daughter's body, whose ends were already cold. She sobbed:

"You would not have died if I had come to you. O murderer, you have let her die of set purpose. You did not want to give her the four or five thousand ounces which her grandfather left her."

He went out, panting like a boar with anger. The mother did not cease to lament her loss: her daughter had been so gentle and so clever. At length the time came to shut down the coffin, and Chou angrily said to his wife:

"You pretend that I let her die so as not to lose four thousand ounces? I order you to put all her jewels in the tomb with her. That is more than five thousand ounces, one would think."

They brought in the wu-tso, the Inspector of Corpses, and also his assistant, to verify the death and to help in hearsing her. The keeper of the family graveyard and his brother, the two Chang, were also there to assist in the mournful work.

The time came for the funeral, and the procession went forth from the town. The coffin was placed in a brick tomb, and the first shovels of earth were thrown upon it. Then all returned home. Three feet of cold insensitive earth covered the body of this young beauty, and it had been full of love.

Now the Inspector of Corpses had a worthless fellow named Feng for his assistant. This miserable boy, on coming back from the cemetery in the evening, said to his mother: "An excellent day's work! Tomorrow we shall be rich!"

"And what successful stroke of business have you concluded?"

"To-day we buried the daughter of Chou, and all her jewels were put in the coffin with her. Instead of leaving them to enrich the earth, would it not be better to take them?"

"Think before you do such a terrible thing!" his mother begged. "This is no matter of a mere whipping. Your father wanted to do the same thing twenty years ago. He opened a coffin, and the corpse began to smile at him. Your father died of that in four or five days. My son, do not do it. It is no easy matter."

"Mother," he answered simply, "my mind is made up. Do not waste your breath on me, for that is useless."

He bent over his bed, and took out of it a heavy iron tool.

"O mother, not each person's destiny is the same. I have consulted soothsayers, and they have told me that I shall become rich this year."

He took also an axe, a leather sack, and a dark lantern, which he placed in readiness. Finally he wrapped himself in a great mantle of reeds, for it was the eleventh moon and the snow had begun to fall. He made a sort of hurdle with about ten inter-crossed bamboos, and fastened it behind his mantle so that it should drag along the ground and efface his footprints.

The second watch was sounding when he went out, and all was still bustle and gaiety in the town. But beyond the walls both silence and solitude reigned in the growing cold. The snow was already thick. Who would have ventured out there?

From time to time he turned his head, but no one followed him. At last he reached the wall of the family graveyard and climbed in. Suddenly a dog ran through the tall grass and leaped at him, barking. The thief had prepared a portion of poisoned meat, and threw it to the dog. The beast, being badly fed, smelt it and swallowed it. He still barked a little, but the venom was potent, and he very soon writhed on the ground.

In the keeper's hut, young Chang said to his elder brother:

"The dog has started barking, and then has stopped. Is that not strange? Perhaps it is a thief. You ought to go and see."

The elder brother rose from his hot bed and took up a weapon, grumbling. Then he opened the door and went out. But he was seized by a whirl of cold snow, and called to the dog: "What are you barking for, O animal of the Gods?"

Then he came back and glided under his blankets.

"There is nothing at all. But it is very cold."

From the distant town came the far sound of the gongs and drums of the third watch. Taking heart, Feng went forward in a snow which deadened his steps. He quickly shovelled the fresh earth from the grave, and then lighted his lantern. Its yellow light lit up but a single point. Forcing two long crowbars between the joints, he loosened one brick, and then another. At last the coffin was uncovered. He inserted his pick under the lid, and pried it off and laid it on one side. The corpse was brought to view.

"Small sister," he murmured. "I am only going to borrow a little of your useless wealth. Do not you grudge it me!"

He took the veil from that charming face. The head was covered with ornaments of gold, and also with pearls. He took them all. He was tempted by the fine and silken garments of the corpse. He stripped it.

But suddenly, the body shook itself and pushed the thief away with violence. He uttered a cry of imbecile terror and shrank back. The corpse had sat up and, in that little light, looked at the open tomb, the scattered tools, and her own unclothed body. The wretched lad, obeying instinctive habit, trembled and lied:

"Little sister, I have come to save you."

Naturally, when little Victorious-Immortal had heard the foul Chou's violent words, her despair had made her lose all sign of life. It was for this reason that she had been put in her coffin while still alive. Aroused now by the cold, her first thought was to remember her father's anger. Her only refuge then was the house of her betrothed, and she said: "If you will take me to The Pavilion of the Quick Hedge, you may have a heavy reward."

"That is easy," answered Feng, seeking in vain for how he should escape.

Ought he to kill her? He hardly had the courage after such a shock. He decided to give her back a few clothes. He put the jewels and his implements in the sack, together with the extinguished lantern, and quickly covered the grave with earth again. Then, because the girl was too weak to walk, he took her on his back and went away from that place. But instead of going to Fan's house, he went to his own. His mother opened the door to him, and cried in terror:

"Have you stolen the corpse also?"

"Do not speak so loud," he answered, setting down his burdens.

He went to his bed, and there put little Victorious-Immortal. He drew a knife from his girdle and showed it to the girl:

"Little one, I have some business to settle with you. If we come to an agreement, I will take you to Fan's house. If not, you very well behold this knife, and I shall cut you in two pieces."

"What do you want with me?" she asked.

"You are going to stay here without making a noise and without trying to escape, until I take you to Fan. As for the rest, we will speak of it another time."

"I will do so! I will indeed do so!"

Then the nasty youth led his mother into the next room to calm her a little.

"But what are you going to do?" she asked.

"Do you think we can be safe when she has gone to Fan?"

"I am not going to take her to Fan."

"What are you going to do, then?"

He gave a country laugh, full of suggestion.

Matters so continued until the fifteenth day of the first Moon, the evening of the Feast of Lanterns. Feng went out to see the illuminations, and also to profit by the opportunities for theft which are always afforded in a crowd. The evening wore on, and he had not yet returned, when a shout arose among the neighbors. Feng's mother opened the door to see what was the matter. A fire had broken out near there. In terror, the old woman made haste to carry her furniture into the yard. Profiting by this confusion, the girl slipped through the door; but in the street she did not know which way to turn. At last she found the road to the Ts'ao Gate, and was running in that direction when she lost herself again. However, when at length she asked where The Pavilion of the Quick Hedge might be, she was shown a near way to it.

The attendant was before the door, and she asked him very politely:

"Ten thousand happinesses! Is not this the house of Fan and Erh-lang?"

"Certainly it is, small lady."

"Could you not lead me to him?"

"Assuredly," he answered.

He showed her the way, calling from the door to his masters; but when Erh-lang, in the pale light of the paper lanterns, recognized the white face of his betrothed, he cried out in dismay: "Ghost! Ghost!"

Confident in her love, she advanced toward him piteously repeating:

"Elder brother! Elder brother! I am alive!"

But he kept recoiling in terror, and crying: "Help! Help!"

How could he fail to believe himself in the presence of a ghost, when he had witnessed the funeral, and had, that very evening, encountered the wife of Chou in mourning garments?

As she was about to touch him and, cringing against the wall, he could retreat no further, his terror redoubled. Not knowing what he did, he picked up a heavy stool and struck his dear visitor on the head with it. She fell back, and her head sounded dully on the stone flags.

Fan ran up at the noise of this. He saw the woman on the ground, and his brother holding the stool.

"What have you done?" he cried. "What is the matter? Was it you who killed her?"

"She is a ghost," the other said.

"If she were a ghost, she would not bleed. What have you done?"

Already some ten persons had come up to see what was the matter. The street guard came in to them and seized Erh-lang, who kept on saying: "She is the ghost of Chou's daughter. I have killed her."

Hearing this name, a neighbor ran to inform Chou, who would not at first believe him. At length he decided to go to the wine pavilion, where he was compelled to recognize her, though he kept on saying:

"I buried her long since!"

Nevertheless, the guard insisted upon leading Erh-lang to prison. Fan had the doors shut then, and stayed with Chou by the corpse till morning.

Early next day the Governor inquired into the matter. The coffin was opened. It was found empty, and the keepers told how their dog had been found dead in the snow on the day after the funeral. In the absence of any completer explanation, they proceeded with their inquiry.

Erh-lang, in his prison, was overcome with sorrowful remorse. Sometimes he said that she could not have survived her burial; sometimes he was rent with horror at the thought that she had been alive when he struck her. He recalled her beauty and grace in Spring by the lake side, and bitter tears rolled from him. While he was musing in this way, he saw his cell door open, and the girl appeared. In his emotion and fear, he cried:

"Are you not dead, my darling?"

"Your blow caused me more grief than harm. Now I have wakened, and have come to see you."

She approached the bench where he sat, and he took her hand:

"How can I have been so foolish as to fear you?"

They were talking thus, and already, in their deep love, they were in each other's arms. His joy was so keen that suddenly he woke. It was a dream.

On the second night the same thing happened, and on the third, and his passion grew stronger for her. As she was going away the third time, she said:

"My life on earth had come to an end, but my love was so great and so potently called me to you, that the Marshal-of- the-Five-Ways, the Keeper-of-the-Frontier-of-the-Shadows, allowed me to come back to you, for these three nights. I must leave you now. But, if you do not forget, there will yet be something of me bound to your soul."

Then she disappeared, and the young man sobbed most bitterly.

In the end the matter was cleared up by chance. Feng's mother, having filched a golden trifle from her son's bag, went to sell it to the same jeweler who had made it for Chou. On being denounced before the Governor, mother and son were apprehended, and all the jewels were discovered in their house. Torture found them words, and the whole matter became clear. Erh-lang had actually believed that he saw a ghost, and was released. Feng was sentenced to slow death, and strips were torn one by one from his body by the executioner. His mother was only strangled.

As for Erh-lang, his heart stayed faithful to the girl he had so greatly loved. At every feast he went to the temple of the Marshal-of-the-Five-Ways, and burned incense, so that the pleasant smoke of it might ascend to the palace of the soul of little Victorious-Immortal. His fidelity touched even the rough heart of Chou and, when he came to die a few years later, his body was buried in the same tomb with her whom his arms had known only in sleep.

A Strange Destiny

Nao fan lou to effing sheng hsien (Chou Victorious-Immortal, of abundant love, overthrows the Pavilion of the Fan). Using shih heng yen (1621), 14th Tale.

THE ERROR OF THE EMBROIDERED SLIPPER

The sun is in our eyes
And we think we are running out towards joy;
Our heart pulls us down
And we shall never know the way of the sky
Or the end of all things.

During the Hung-Chih period of our dynasty there lived at Hang-chow a young man who was called Chang Loyalty. After his parents died, leaving him a great fortune, he no longer had anyone to guide him, and therefore, throwing away his books, he spent his time with gallants of the sort we name fou-lang-tzu, that is to say "floating-on-the-waves." They do not know how to profit by opportunity. So Chang no longer studied anything but various ball games, he abandoned himself to the pleasures of the theatre, and took his delight in those gardens where the breezes of love blow in the moonlight. In a word, he followed the changing flowers of illusion; and, as he was himself seductive, as impassioned as expert in pleasure, and rich and generous, he became the favorite of all the women of the town. One day, when spring had but just caused all the flowers to come out on the amiable banks of the Lake of the West,

Chang invited a company of singing girls and idlers to spend the afternoon on the blue waters.

He put on a gauze bonnet with floating wings, after the fashion of the time. His great transparent silk robe was of purple and silver, over a second embroidered one of pure white. White gauze stockings and red slippers completed the elegance of his appearance.

He went out, walking unhurriedly, gently waving a fan decorated with paintings. Behind him walked his little slave, Clear-Lute, who carried over his shoulder a mantle in case the weather should freshen, and a long guitar with which to accompany the singing girls.

As they were approaching the gate of Ch'ien-t'ang, Chang looked up, for no particular reason. On the first story of a house a maiden held back her window curtain and looked at him. From her whole person emanated so troubling a charm that he stopped in his walk, and felt a tremor in his body. For a long time they remained gazing at each other, until she slowly broke into a smile, and he felt his soul fly from him.

At this moment the door of the house opened below, and a man came forth; so Chang hastened to resume his walk, and returned in a few moments. The curtain was drawn back over the window. He waited, but there was no sign. At length he drew away, turning his head, and walking as slowly as if he had already gone a hundred leagues on the mountains.

Yet eventually he passed the town gate and rejoined his friends on the boat, which was at once steered to the middle of the lake. The banks were smiling with peach blossom: the willow leaves were a mist of gold and green. Little boats, with brightly-dressed passengers, crossed and re-crossed like ants. In very truth:

Hills are heaped upon hills
And the pavilions on the pavilions.
The songs and dances are never ceasing
On the West Lake.
The warm breeze fans the drunkenness
Of the pleasure walkers.
Heaven is above,
But here toe have Hang-chow and So-chow Lakes.

But Chang carried the picture of that young girl in his soul, and had no heart for pleasure.

His companions offered him cups of wine, wondering at his melancholy; but he was far from them.

At twilight they returned, and Chang re-entered by the Ch'ien-t'ang gate, passing before the girl's house. The window was shut. He stopped, and forced a cough; but there was no sign. He went to the end of the street, and came back again, but all was silent. Therefore he had no choice but to go away.

He returned next morning, and stayed at a shop near by to learn what he could. He was told:

"They are people called P'an. Their only daughter is sixteen years of age, and is named Eternal Life. The father has some connection with a certain powerful family which affords him protection. He lives by swindling, and everyone fears him. He is a veritable skin-pinker and bravo."

This news made Chang a little thoughtful, but he walked on by the house nevertheless. The young girl was again at her window. They looked at each other; but there were people about, and he had to go away.

That evening, as soon as night fell, he went back. The moon was shining as brightly as the sun, and the street was empty. The youthful beauty leaned at her window, wrapped in thought and bathed in the white light. She smiled at him, and he drew from his sleeve his scarlet muslin handkerchief. He made the knot known as "union of hearts gives victory." Rolling it in a ball, he threw it, and she adroitly caught it in two hands. Then she stooped and took off one of her little embroidered slippers. She dropped it into Chang's waiting fingers. Enraptured with this gift, which was a pledge of love and faith, he carried it to his lips and said softly:

"Thank you! Thank you, with all my heart!"
In tones of maddening sweetness, she replied:
"Ten thousand happinesses!"

Just then a rough voice was heard within the house. She made another sign to him and closed the window. And he went home drunk through silent streets made silver by the moon. Once in his library, he examined the slipper. It was a golden lotus, so small and so light that a thousand thoughts troubled the lover. He said:

"I must find someone to arrange our meeting, or else die from an over-stressing of desire."

Early in the morning, he put some pieces of silver in his sleeve and hastened to a little wine booth, not far from the house of P'an. He knew that he would find an old woman there, whom he often met in pleasurable places. In fact, he saw her and called to her. She at once saluted him, saying:

"Aya! My uncle, what brings you?"

"I happened to be passing," he answered carelessly. "But I should like you to walk a little way with me."

"In what can I serve you?" she hastened to ask.

Without speaking, he took her into a quiet little tavern. When they were seated, and the attendant had brought them fruit and dishes of food, he poured out a full cup of hot wine and offered it to her, saying:

"I have something to ask of you, ma-ma Lu. But I am afraid that you cannot accomplish it."

"Without boasting," she answered with a wide smile, "there are few enterprises, however difficult, in which I do not succeed. What is it you desire?"

"I want you to arrange a meeting for me with the daughter of P'an, who lives in the Street of the Ten Officials. Here are five ounces of silver to begin with. If you succeed, you shall have quite as much more."

"The small Eternal Life? The little witch! I thought her so demure! I should never have imagined she was a wild flower. But the matter is difficult. There are only the parents and the daughter in that house, and the father in dangerous. He keeps a damnably suspicious watch over his door. How could you get in? I dare not promise any success."

"You have just boasted that you always succeed. Here are two ounces more."

The old woman's eyes gleamed like fire at the sight of the snow-colored metal, and she said:

"I will take the risk. If all goes well, it will be your fortune. If not, I shall at least have done my best. But give me a proof, for otherwise she would not listen to me."

Not without regret, Chang took from his bosom the little slipper, and gave it to her, wrapped in his handkerchief. The old woman at once slipped it into her sleeve with the pieces of money. As she was leaving him, she said again:

"The affair is delicate. You must have patience and not hurry me. That would be dangerous."

"I only ask you to do your best. Come and tell me as soon as you have an answer."

Eternal Life was profoundly agitated. Since that moonlit night she had had no more taste for food, but had said:

"If I married him I would not have lived in vain. But I know neither his name nor where he lives. When I saw him beneath the moon, why had I not wings to fly to him?... As it is, I had only this red handkerchief,"

Yet she had to live and speak as usual. But as soon as she was alone she fell again into her musing.

Two days later, old Lu entered their house. The father had gone out. The visitor said to mother and daughter:

"I received certain artificial flowers yesterday, and have come to show them to you."

She took a bunch of a thousand shades out of her basket.

"Would you not say they were real?"

"When I was young," said the mother, "we only wore ordinary flowers, and did not dream of marvels like these."

"Yet these are only considered mediocre. But the price of the finest is so high."

"If we cannot buy them, we can at least admire them," the young woman answered dryly.

With gathering smiles, the old woman took from the basket a bunch which was indeed incomparable.

"And what is the price of that?" questioned the mother.

"How should I dare to fix a price? I leave it to you. But if you have a little tea, I would willingly drink of it."

"In the admiration caused by your flowers, we have forgotten our manners. Wait for one moment, while I fetch some boiling water."

As soon as the mother had left the room, the woman took a slight parcel from her sleeve.

"What have you there?" asked Eternal Life.

"Something important which you must not see."

"Oh, but I must see it then."

"I shall not give it to you," said the cunning old woman. "Aya! You have taken it from me by force!" she added, letting the parcel into the girl's hand.

Impatiently the child untied the handkerchief, and recognized the slipper. Her face flushed into scarlet, and she said with difficulty: "A single one of these objects is of no use, ma-ma. Why did you show it me?"

"I know a certain Lord who would give his life to have the pair. Will you not consent to help me?"

Trembling all over, Eternal Life said to her softly:

"Since you know all, tell me his name and where he lives."

"He is called Chang, and he owns a hundred myriads of ounces. He is very gentle; his love is as deep as the sea. He has lost his soul through thinking of you, and has bidden me arrange a means for his entry."

"How can it be done? My father is terrible. When I have blown out my lamp, he often comes to look into the rooms. What is your plan, ma-ma?"

The old woman thought for a minute, and then said:

"It is not very difficult. You must go to bed early and, as soon as your father has come up and gone down again, you must rise quietly and open the window. You must wait for a signal, and let down a long piece of cloth. He will climb up with the help of this rope, and, if he is careful to go away before the fifth watch, no one will surprise you."

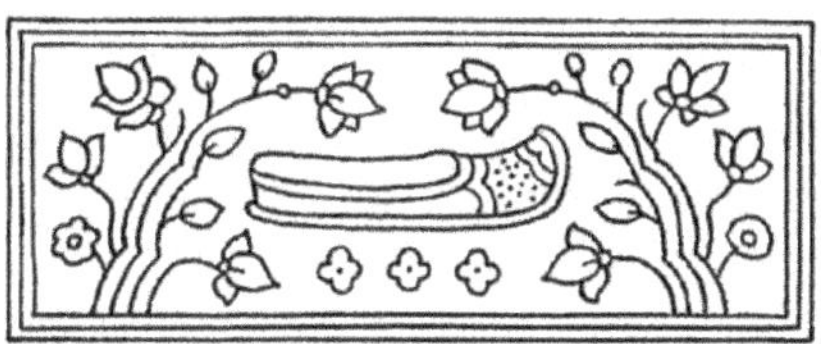

"Admirable!" cried the delighted child. "When will he come?"

"It is too late to-day. But I will go to him to-morrow morning. Give me a pledge of re-assurance for him."

"Assuredly! Take the other slipper. He will give it back to me to-morrow."

The old woman hid it in her sleeve, for the mother came in by this time with the tea. Soon after, she took up her basket and went away, accompanied to the door by the two women.

She went straight to the house of Chang, but he was out. She offered her flowers to the women of the house, waiting for some part of the day in vain.

Next morning she went again to find the young man, but he had not returned. She went away thoughtful.

The truth is that Chang had remained three days in the house of a Flower-in-the-Mist. When he returned and heard of the old woman's two visits, he hastened to find her. She said to him:

"The pledge of love which you entrusted to me is in her hand. She bade me tell you that her father is dangerous, but that he is to be away for a long time shortly. She will inform us." On his return journey the young man passed by P'an's house. Eternal Life was at her window, and they smiled tenderly at one another.

* * *

Three months had passed. Chang was sitting one morning in his library, when his servants told him that four police officers had come with a summons. He asked himself fearfully whether he had been mixed up in any scandal at a pleasure house; but he had to obey. He questioned the officers.

"It is a matter of taxes and duties," they answered.

Reassured, he changed his clothes and went with them, followed by several of his servants. He was taken at once to the hall where the Court sat, and, standing before the red table, he saluted the magistrate. The latter looked at him intently, and harshly asked:

"How did you enter into an intrigue with P'an's daughter? How did you kill her father and her mother?"

Chang was a libertine. That is to say he had neither strength nor energy. Hearing himself thus unexpectedly accused of a double crime, he shook from head to foot, as if a bolt had fallen on him from a calm sky. He stammered:

"Although I had the intention of establishing a connection with her, I have not yet succeeded in doing so. As yet I have not known her house."

The Governor thundered:

"She has just confessed that her relation with you has lasted several months. How dare you deny it?"

Just then Chang perceived that the young girl was kneeling close to him. Bewildered and not knowing what to do, he turned to Eternal Life and asked:

"How can you say that I have been intimate with you? With what object are you trying to encompass my ruin?"

She sobbed without answering. Meanwhile the Governor called upon the officers to apply the buskin of torture to the young man. And they swarmed about him like ants.

Unhappily for him, Chang Loyalty had been brought up in muslin and gauze, and had grown to manhood in a brocade. How could he endure such torture? Hardly had he felt the pressure of the buskin before he cried:

"I confess everything!"

The Governor had a brush and paper given to the accused, that he might himself write out his confession. The unhappy man wept, saying:

"What must I write? I know nothing of the matter!" Then he turned to the young girl and added: "Do you at least tell me what you have done, so that I may write my confession."

Eternal Life answered in irritation: "Did you not look at me with lecherous eyes under my window? Did you not throw your handkerchief? Did you not match the pair of my embroidered slippers?"

"All that is true. But about the rest?"

The Governor here interrupted:

"If one thing is true, the rest is also. What is the use of arguing? Since he refuses to write, let him be given thirty strokes of the heavy bamboo, let him be cast into the cell for those who are condemned to death."

Happily for Chang, his gaolers knew that he was very rich. They but touched him with their blows, and led him to prison with as much care as they would a butterfly. Each of them cried: "Uncle, how could you do such a thing?" "O my elder brothers," he lamented, "if it is true that I desired this girl, yet have I never met her. Do you believe that I could be a murderer? I know nothing about the murder. Tell me of it."

So he learned that, this very morning, Eternal Life on waking up had been surprised by the silence of the house. From the ground-floor room where she had passed the night, she had gone up to the story where her parents slept, and had opened the door of their room. In front of the bed, under the half-drawn curtains, the floor was a tarn of blood.

She was so frightened that she tumbled down the stairs and fell upon the street door, sobbing and crying out. Neighbors heard her and ran up, and she said to them:

"Yesterday, my parents went up to their room. I do not know who has killed them both."

The bolder ones went up the stairs to see. They opened the bed-curtains, and there were the man and his wife, stiff and with their throats cut across. They looked to right and left. The window was shut, and nothing was disturbed.

"It is a serious matter," they muttered. "Let us not act hastily."

One of them went at once to warn the district chief of police, who came and examined the scene of the crime. He shut and sealed the house, and led Eternal Life to the Governor's Court. The girl knelt down and told all that she knew, and the Governor said:

"If the door and windows were closed, and nothing has been stolen, the matter is dubious. Had your father an enemy?"

"Not to my knowledge."

"That is strange!" murmured the Governor, and thought for a moment.

Suddenly he told the officers to take off the silken veil with which the young girl had half-covered her head. He could then see her exceptional beauty.

"How old are you? Are you not betrothed?"

"I am seventeen, and I am still free."

"And you sleep on the ground-floor, while your parents have their room above? That is very curious."

"Until quite recently your slave slept above. But fifteen days ago they made a change. I do not know why."

The judge again reflected. Then he struck the table violently, crying out:

"It is you who have killed your father and mother. Or, rather, it is your lover. Tell me his name."

"Your slave never leaves the house. How could she have a forbidden love? Would not the neighbors know it?"

The judge made a salacious grimace:

"In a case of murder the neighbors know nothing. It is clear that you have had relations with a man. Your parents knew of it, and that is why they changed their room. Your lover killed them in a rage."

Hearing these words, she became scarlet and then pale. At a sign from the Governor, the gaolers threw themselves like tigers upon the little girl, closing a cruel pair of iron nippers on her pellucid and delicate jade hand. As the jaws began to crush her fingers, she uttered loud cries: "Mercy, my lord. I have a lover." "What is his name?" "Chang Loyalty."

And then she fainted. The Governor knew enough. He summoned the young man and, being convinced of his guilt, had him put in prison, while awaiting further information. It is well said in a certain proverb "Even while you are sitting in your house with the doors shut, misfortune falls from heaven."

In prison, Chang reflected upon this sudden accusation. Could he have committed this double crime in his sleep? In the end he offered his gaolers ten ounces if they would take him to Eternal Life. When they bargained, he promised twenty ounces. Then they led him as far as the grill of the woman's prison. The girl was there, weeping without stint. As soon as she saw him, she reviled him between her sobs:

"Ungrateful and dishonorable! You made me mad with love for you. Why should you cut my parents' throats, and cause my death?"

"Do not make unnecessary noise," he interrupted. "Let us rather try to clear up this mystery. It is certain that I sent the old woman Lu to you with your little slipper. Did you see her?"

"Naturally, wretch," she answered disdainfully.

Again he interrupted:

"She told me that you had kept your pledge, that your father was terrible, and that you were awaiting his departure in order to arrange a meeting. But since then I have known nothing of you, save a few rare smiles."

"Forgetful murderer," she groaned, "again you deny it. Did you not confess all before the judge? Why do you come to torment me?"

"My unfortunate body could not endure the torture. By confessing I gained some days of life. Do not fly into a rage, but answer me: what happened after ma-ma Lu had visited you?"

"We arranged everything for the next night. You came and gave me back my slipper. Since then you have climbed up to my room each night. Dare you say it is not true?"

Chang thought deeply. The bystanders wondered whether he were guilty and seeking a clever explanation to save himself, or whether he were really innocent. At last he said: "Then if we have met often, you should be very certain of my voice and body. Look at me well, and think."

The gaolers exclaimed:

"What he says is just. If there were a mistake, would you leave him to die?"

Eternal Life was puzzled, and looked at him earnestly. He repeated:

"Is it I? Dear heart, speak quickly!"

"He who came," she said at last, "was perhaps bigger. But it was always dark, and how can I be sure? But I remember that on your left shoulder you have a scar as big as a copper piece."

The bystanders at once exclaimed:

"That is easy to verify. There can be no further mistake. Uncle, unclothe yourself quickly. If there is nothing there, we shall inform the Governor."

Chang immediately uncovered his shoulder, and the white flesh was as smooth as marble. Eternal Life could not believe her eyes. When the young man had gone back, filled full of hope, to his prison, the gaolers made their report to the Governor, who had already summoned ma-ma Lu.

In the audience chamber the old woman knelt down and was quite overcome. The judge began by ordering her forty strokes for having acted as an abettor of corruption. The flesh of her thighs was nothing but a bloody paste. She told the whole story.

After coming back from Chang's house without having seen him, old Lu had found her son Wu-han in their little food shop. He had said to her:

"You come at the right time. I must kill a pig this morning, and our assistant has gone out for the day."

The old woman did not like this work. But she was very much afraid of her son, and did not dare to refuse. "Wait till I have changed my clothes!" was all she said. While she was taking off her outer garment, a parcel fell from the sleeve of it. Thinking, that it was money, Wu-han quickly picked it up and opened it. It was the pair of embroidered slippers. He said:

"Oh! Oh! Who is the little girl who has such feet? She must be of a very loving nature. If I could hold her to my heart for a whole night, I should not have lived in vain. But how do these slippers come here, for they have already been worn?"

"Give them back to me!" she cried. "There is much money in them, which I will hand to you." And she told him the whole matter. But he objected:

"It has been a common saying from the earliest times that acts not committed can alone remain unknown. This P'an is a bravo. If he learns of the matter, all the silver which you receive will be too little to buy his silence. Our whole shop would fall into his hands." In dismay the old woman replied:

"Your words are full of reason. I am going to give back the silver and the slippers. I am going to let it be understood that I refuse to embroil myself with curtain affairs."

"Where is the silver?" he asked.

The old woman took it from her sleeve, and he put it into his, saying:

"Leave all to me. If they should happen to come and seek a quarrel with us, we shall have proofs against them. And, if nothing comes of it, no one will dare to reclaim the money."

"But what shall I say if he asks me for news?"

"That you have not had time enough. Or even that the matter cannot be arranged."

What could she do, she who was thus deprived of the money and the pledge of love? She was surely obliged to lie.

As for Wu-han, he at once went out and spent the money on rich clothes and a fine gauze bonnet.

In the evening, when his mother was asleep, he put on his pretty clothes and set the slippers in his sleeve. As the great clock sounded the first watch, he went out softly and made straight for the house of P'an. Light clouds were hiding the moon. It was only half full.

He coughed before the house. The window opened, and Eternal Life appeared. She tied a piece of silk to the frame, and let the other end fall. He caught it and climbed up, making use of the projections of the wall with his two feet. Then, with a thousand precautions, he stepped over the sill. Trembling, the girl hastened to draw back the piece of silk and to shut the window.

Then he took the child in his arms, and passion leaped up in their two hearts. In the darkness, and in such emotion, how could that mistake be known? The usurper drew her toward her bed.

Even so is the precious scented flower of the nutmeg embraced by the bind-weed. Even so is the plum blossom torn by the hail. Even so is the sparrow's nest most outraged by the cuckoo.

When the first clouds of their desire were dissipated by the rain of caresses, Wu-han took from his sleeve the pledges of love. She gave them back to him:

"Now that I am happy, I no more wish to go out."

About the fourth watch, before daylight, Wu-han arose and climbed stealthily down to the street.

Since that time there had to be a storm of rain, or the moon had to be very clear, to prevent Wu-han from hurrying to the small woman. The days, and then the months, passed in this way.

One night the deceiver accidentally made some noise as he went away. P'an immediately came up to them, but saw nothing; for Eternal Life succeeded in not betraying herself. Next night she warned her lover, saying to him in her sense:

"Do not come for a few days. That will be safer. Let us give them time to forget about it."

But her father had his ears on the alert; he heard the window creak, and he ran up, though again too late. In the morning he said to his wife:

"This baby is certainly about some villainy. She keeps her mouth as tight as a trap."

"I also have a suspicion," replied her mother.

"Yet the room opens on to the stairs, which come down into our room."

"I am going to give her a good taste of the rod to make her speak."

"That is a bad plan, a very bad plan," said her mother. "It is a true proverb that you must not show family blemishes. If you beat her, all the neighbors will know, and who would wish to marry her? Let us rather make her sleep in our room, which has no way out except the door. We will spend the night up the stairs, and see what happens."

On being told of this proposal, Eternal Life dared not say anything. And on the higher floor husband and wife slept in peace.

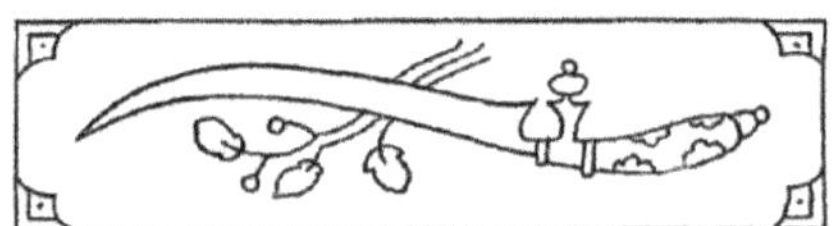

One evening Wu-han felt his heart seething with passion. Fearing that he might be attacked by P'an, he armed himself with a knife, which he used to cut pigs' throats. Under Eternal Life's window, he coughed softly. Nothing stirred. He coughed more loudly, thinking she was asleep. But everything remained quiet. He was going back to his house, in a thoughtful mood, when he saw a ladder left near to a house which was being built. He seized upon it, carried it away, and put it up against Eternal Life's window. The catch was not locked. He pushed it open, climbed over the sill, and silently went toward the bed.

Drunken with joy, Wu-han was already disrobing himself of his clothes, when, in the stillness of the night, his ears caught the sound of two people breathing, instead of one. He listened with controlled breath. Unmistakably the rough breathing of a man was mingled with the softer murmur of a woman.

He was suddenly blinded with violent anger:

"This is why she did not answer my signal. The vile child has another man in bed. It was to get rid of me that she told me of her father's suspicion!"

In his jealous madness he drew his knife and gently felt for the man's throat. With a clean blow he drove the weapon into the flesh, and before the woman could move, he cut her throat also, almost beheading her.

He wiped the knife and his hands on the blanket, opened the window, and descended. He had closed the catches. Once outside, he ran to replace the ladder, and went back to his house. Denounced by his mother and brought before the Court, Wu-han tried to deny the accusation. But the officers, on uncovering his shoulder, brought a scar to view. Eternal Life recognized his voice and his body. The first torture overcame his obstinacy, and he confessed all.

The murderer was condemned to slow death.

Eternal Life was strangled, as was old Lu.

Chang, whose lecherous intentions had been the cause of all, was sentenced to a heavy fine. In dismay, and half ruined, he no more left his study chamber. Not long afterwards, he was carried off by a lassitude and a languor.

Lu Wu-han yin liu ho chin hsieh (Lu Wu-han keeps an Embroidered Slipper to his scathe)
Hsing Shih heng yen (1627), 16th Tale.

THE COUNTERFEIT OLD WOMAN

During the Ch'eng-Hua period of our dynasty, there lived at Shantung a young man named Flowering Mulberry, whose parents possessed a sufficient fortune. He had just bound up his hair beneath his man's bonnet; his fresh and rosy complexion added to the delicate charm of his features.

One day, as he was going to visit an uncle in a neighboring village, he was overtaken on the way by a heavy storm of rain, and ran for shelter into a disused temple; and there, seated on the ground waiting for the rain to stop, was an old woman. Flowering Mulberry sat down and, since the storm grew more violent, resigned himself to wait.

Finding him beautiful, the old woman began to converse and ingratiate herself with him, until at length she came across to him, and finally her hands wandered gently over his body.

He found this an agreeable manner of passing the time, but said after a little while: "How is it that, although you are a woman, you have the voice of a man?"

"My son, I will tell you the truth, but you must not reveal it to anybody. I am not really a woman, but a man.

When I was little, I used often to disguise myself and mimic the shrill tones of young girls; and I even learned to sew just as well as they. I used often to go to the neighboring market towns, pretending that I was a young girl and offering to do needlework; and my skill was soon much admired by all the dwellers in the houses where I worked.

"I used to go to bed with the women, and by degrees, according to the licentiousness of their thought, we would enjoy our pleasure. Soon the women found that they had no more occasion to go out for their dalliance; and even the sober-minded girls among them became involved. They did not dare to say anything, for fear of the scandal; and also I had a drug which I applied during the night to their faces, stupefying them so that they allowed me to do as I liked. When they recovered their senses it was too late, and they dared not protest. On the contrary, they used to bribe me with gold and silken stuffs to keep silence and to leave their house. Ever since then—and I am now forty-seven years of age—I have never again put on a man's garments. I have traveled throughout the two capitals and the nine provinces, and always when I see a beautiful woman I contrive to go to her house. In this way I accumulate riches with but little labor; and I have never been found out."

"What an astonishing tale!" cried the fascinated Flowering Mulberry. "I wonder whether I could do the like."

"One as beautiful as you are," answered the other, "will be taken for a woman by everyone. If you wish me to be your instructor you have only to come with me. I will bind up your feet, and teach you to sew; and we will go into every house together. You shall be my niece. If we find a good opportunity I shall give you a little of my drug, and you will then have no difficulty in achieving your purpose."

The young man's heart was devoured by a desire to put this adventure to the proof. Without further hesitation he prostrated himself four times, and adopted the old woman as his master, taking not a moment's thought for his parents or for his honor. Such an intoxicating thing is vice.

When it had stopped raining, he set out with the old woman; and as soon as they were beyond the boundaries of Shantung they purchased hair-pins and feminine dresses. The disguise was perfect, and anyone would have sworn that Flowering Mulberry was an authentic woman. He changed his first name for that of Niang "the little girl," though for a few days he was so embarrassed that he did not dare to speak.

But his master seemed no longer wishful to look for fresh victims. Every evening he insisted upon his niece sharing his bed; and up to a very late hour would proceed with his instruction and that even to the furthest detail.

It was not for this that Flowering Mulberry had disguised himself. One day he declared that thenceforward each should go his own way, and the other was bound to agree; but before leaving him, he gave the boy some further advice:

"Two highly important rules are to be observed in our profession. The first is not to stop too long in the same house.

If you stayed in the one place more than half a month, you would certainly be discovered. Therefore often change your district, so that from month to month there may be no time for the traces of your passage to become noticeable. The second rule is not to let a man come near you. You are beautiful, young and alone in life, and they will all wish to interfere with you. Therefore always surround yourself with women. One last word: have nothing to do with little girls; for they cry out and weep."

So then the two parted.

In the first village he came to, Flowering Mulberry perceived through a door the silhouette of a most graceful young woman, and struck upon the door by its copper knocker. The girl opened, and looked at him through eyes filled with fire. A needle-woman was just what they required.

But in the evening the boy was disappointed by the arrival of a husband, whose lusty appearance left him small hope for the night.

He was forced to wait until the young woman was left alone in the house by day, and came to work in the chamber where he sat. Then he ventured an observation upon the appearance of the countryside, and afterwards congratulated her on her husband. She blushed, and their conversation became more intimate. It was not until the next day, however, that he dared to make an advance. This met with immediate success. Two days afterwards he was forced into a hurried departure; for the husband had taken notice of him, and profited by his wife's momentary absence to suggest caresses.

Thenceforward he followed his trade. At the age of thirty-two he had travelled over more than half the empire, and had beguiled several thousand women. Often, he was so bold as to attack more than eight persons at a time, in a single house, and not even the little slaves escaped his attention. The happiness of which he was thus the cause remained unsuspected, and no one suffered by it, since none could dream of its existence. He always remembered his master's rule, and never risked staying for more than a few days in the same place.

At last he came to the province West-of-the-River, and was received into an important house, where there were more than fifteen women, all beautiful and young. His feeling toward each of these was of so lively a nature that twenty days had passed before he could make up his mind to go away. Now the husband of one of these girls perceived him and, at once falling in love with him, arranged that his wife should cause him to come to their house. Flowering Mulberry went, suspecting nothing, and hardly had he entered before the man came into the room, took him by the waist and asked for pleasure of him. Naturally he refused and began to cry out; but the husband took not the slightest notice of that. He pushed him on to the bed and undid his garments. But his shameless hands found another matter than that which they expected. It was his turn to cry out: the slaves ran in, bound Flowering Mulberry, and led him to the court of justice. In front of the judge he tried to plead that he had adopted his disguise in order to gain his living. But torture drew from him his real name and the true motive of his behavior, together with an account of his latest exploits.

The Governor sent a report to the higher authorities, for he had no precedent and knew not to what punishment to condemn him. The Viceroy decided that the case must come under the law of adultery, and, also that which dealt with the propagation of immorality. The penalty was a slow death. No extenuating circumstances were admitted. So ended this story.

Hsing shih heng yen (1627), 10th Tale.

THE MONASTERY OF THE ESTEEMED-LOTUS

In the town of Eternal Purity there was once a large monastery dedicated to the Esteemed-Lotus. It contained hundreds of rooms, and its grounds covered several thousand acres. Its wealth and prosperity were due to the possession of a famous relic.

The bonzes, who numbered about a hundred, lived in luxury; and visitors were sure to be received by one of them from the moment of entry, and to be invited to take tea and cakes. Now in the temple there was a "Babies' Chapel," which was reputed to possess miraculous virtue. By passing the night in it and burning incense, women who wished to have a son obtained a son: those who wished for a daughter obtained a daughter.

Round the main hall were set several cells. Women who wished for children had to be of vigorous age and free from malady. They used to fast for seven days, and then go into the temple to prostrate themselves before Fo, and to consult the wands of divination. If the omens were favorable, they passed a night locked up alone in one of the cells, for the purpose of prayer. If the omens were unfavorable, it was because their prayers had not been sufficiently sincere. The bonzes made this fault known to them; and they began their seven days' fast anew, before returning to make their devotions.

The cells had no sort of opening in their walls, and when a penitent entered one of them, her family and attendants used to come and install her. As soon as night came, she was locked in the cell, and the bonzes insisted that a member of her family must pass the night before her door, so that none might entertain the least suspicion of an entry to her. When the woman returned to her home, the child was already formed. It was born fat and beautiful always, and without any blemish.

There was, moreover, no household, either of public officials or the common people, which did not send one or even two of its members to pray in the Babies' Chapel. And women came to it even from the provinces.

Every day the crowd in the monastery was comparable with mountains or the sea, and the place was filled with the gayest hubbub. They no longer kept any reckoning of the offerings of every kind which flowed in upon them. When the women were asked how, during the night, the P'u-sa had made his answer intelligible, some answered simply that Fo had told them in a dream that they would have a son. Others said that they had dreamed that a lo-han had come and lain beside them. Others asserted that they had had no dream.

Others again blushed and declined to answer. Some women never repeated this kind of prayer a second time: others, on the contrary, went to the temple as often as possible.

You will tell me that this story of a Fo or of a P'u-sa coming every night to the monastery is in no way short of preposterous. But it must be borne in mind that the people of that district had a greater faith in sorcerers than in doctors, and could not distinguish the true from the false.

Consequently they continued to send their wives to the temple.

As a matter of course these bonzes, whose outward behavior was so laudable and correct, were wholly and unreservedly gluttons within, both for luxury and debauch.

Although the cells were apparently quite close, each really had a secret door. When the women were sound asleep, the bonzes came softly into the cell, and to such purpose that, when their victims were aroused, it was already almost too late. Those who would have wished to protest kept silence for the sake of their reputations.

Now the women were young and sound: the bonzes were strong and vigorous. They had, moreover, taken the precaution to cause certain special pills to be administered to their visitors. Consequently it but rarely happened that these prayers were not heard. Sober-minded wives would have died with shame sooner than confess the matter to their husbands; and, as for the others, they kept quiet so that they might be able to do it again.

Matters were in this case when a new Governor was appointed to the district, the Lord Wang. Soon after he entered upon his office, he heard tell of the Monastery of the Esteemed-Lotus, and could not help thinking:

"Since it is Fo and P'u-sa who are involved, it should be enough simply to pray. Why, then, must the women also go and pass the night in the temple? There must be some questionable artifice in that."

But he could do nothing without proof; so he waited until the ninth Sun of the ninth Moon, which was a great festival, and then mixed with the crowd of the faithful who went to the holy place.

Passing through the main gate, he found himself beneath great acacias and hundred-year-old pines. Before him stood the temple, brightly painted with vermilion and decorated by a tablet on which was inscribed in gold letters: "Monastery of the Esteemed-Lotus, for Retirement." To right and left was a succession of pavilions, and innumerable visitors were going out and coming in.

The first bonze who saw the Governor wished to run and warn his companions. The Lord Wang attempted to stop him, but he broke loose, and soon the drums and bells were sounding to do honor to the magistrate, while the bonzes formed in two ranks and bowed as he passed along.

He entered the temple and burned some joss-sticks; after which the Superior made him a low obeisance and begged him to come and rest himself for a moment in the reception hall. Tea was served. Then, concealing his true design, the Governor said:

"I have learned of the great reputation of this Holy Retreat, and I intend to ask the Emperor to grant you a tablet of honor inscribed with the names and particulars of all the bonzes of the district."

Naturally the delighted Superior wished to prostrate himself in thanks; but the Governor continued:

"They have spoken to me also of a miraculous chapel. Is the matter so in truth? And in what manner are these prayers made?"

The Superior answered without misgiving that the period of fasting was seven days; but that by reason of the greatness of their desire and the sincerity of their prayers it most frequently happened that the petitions of the suppliants were granted in a dream during the night which they passed at the monastery.

The Governor asked carelessly what measures were taken to ensure the preservation of the proprieties; and the other explained that the cells had no other entrance than the door, before which a member of the family, had to pass the night.

"Since that is the case," said the visitor, "I shall send my wife here."

"If you wish for a son, it is only necessary for both of you to pray sincerely in your palace, and the miracle will be accomplished," the Superior assured him hastily; for he was greatly afraid to see the local authorities concerning themselves in this affair.

"But why must the wives of the people come here, if my wife need not disturb herself to do so?"

"Are you not the protector of our doctrine, and is it not natural that the spirits should pay special attention to your prayers?" answered the astute bonze.

"So be it," agreed Wang. "But allow me to visit this miraculous chapel."

The hall was filled with women, who fled to right and left. The statue of Kwan-yin was covered with necklaces and pieces of embroidery. She was represented holding a child in her arms, while four or five babies clung to her robe. The altar and the walls were covered with votive offerings, chiefly consisting of embroidered slippers. Candles beyond number were held in branches of candlesticks. The hall was filled with the smoke of incense. To the left was the immortal Chang who gives us children. To the right was the "Officer of the Star of Extended Longevity."

Wang bowed before the goddess. Then he went to visit the penitents' cells. Each ceiling was painted over with flowers, a carpet covered each floor and the bed, the table and the chairs were spotlessly clean.

He examined the cells carefully all over and found no crack. Not a mouse, not even an ant could have entered in. He went out in perplexity and, after the usual formalities, again stepped into his palankeen, which was accompanied to the gate by all the bonzes.

Thinking to the right and musing to the left, as the proverb says, the Governor suddenly conceived a plan. As soon as he arrived at the palace, he summoned one of his secretaries, and said to him:

"Go and find me two harlots, and clothe them as honest women. Give one of them a box of black ink and the other a box of vermilion paste, and send them to pass the night at the monastery. If any one approaches them, let them mark his head with the red and the black. I shall go myself to-morrow morning to examine the matter. Above all, let this thing be kept the closest secret."

The secretary at once went to seek out two public women of his acquaintance. One was named Mei-chieh, and the other Wan-erh. He took them to his house, explained the Governor's orders to them, and clothed them as matrons of good family. He summoned two palankeens, which he caused the sham penitents to enter, and himself conducted the procession to the monastery. He left the women in their cells, and came back to inform the monk on duty.

After his departure, a little novice brought tea to the present visitors, who were more than ten in number. Who would have thought of troubling to examine the two new arrivals?

At the sounding of the first watch, all the cells were locked. The members of the various families took up their positions before the doors. The bonzes shut themselves into their own apartments.

When Mei-chieh found herself alone, she put her little box of vermilion near the pillow, turned up the lamp, undressed herself, and lay upon the bed. But she was unable to sleep for thinking of her mission, and continually kept looking through the bed curtains.

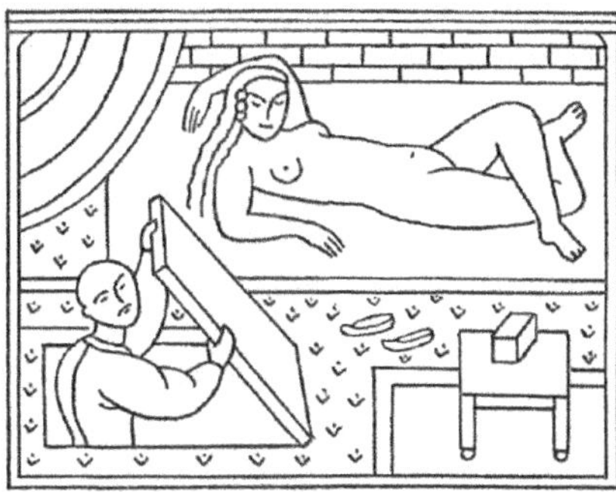

The second watch sounded. On every side the sounds of human life were silenced, and all things were still. Suddenly she heard, under the floor, this noise: Ko-Ko. She sat up, thinking it was a rat, and saw a part of the floor move to one side. A shaven head appeared, and was quickly followed by the whole body. It was a bonze. Mei-chieh was astounded, and thought:

"So these rascally priests have been outraging honest women!"

But she did not stir. The bonze quietly blew out the lamp, came towards the bed, let fall his robe, and slipped under the blankets.

Mei-chieh pretended to be asleep. She felt him gently move her leg to one side, and then she made as though to wake saying:

"Who are you who come in the night and insult me?" She pushed him away, but the bonze embraced her in his arms, and whispered: "I am a lo-han with a body of gold, and I have come to give you a son."

While speaking, he busied himself in accordance with his salacity. It must be said that all bonzes have no mean talent in the matter of cloud and rain; and this one was full of vigorous manhood. Mei-chieh was a woman of great experience, but she was unable to resist him and had difficulty, at length, in repressing her sighs. However, she took advantage of his arriving at the supreme point of his emotion to dip her fingers in the box of vermilion and to mark his head without his perceiving it. After a certain time, the bonze glided from the bed, leaving the girl a little packet, and saying:

"Here are some pills to assist your prayer. Take three-tenths of an ounce each day in hot water, and you will have a son."

Weary in body, Mei-chieh was just dimly closing her eyes, when she was aroused by a fresh touch, and, thinking that the same bonze had returned, said in surprise:

“What? Are you able to come back again, when even I am so tired?”

But he answered without a pause:

“You are making a mistake! I have but just come, and the savour of my comforts is as yet unknown to you.”

“But, I am tired...." "In that case, take one of these pills...”

And he handed her a packet. But she was afraid that it might be poison and placed it on the bed, contriving in the same movement to dip her fingers in the vermilion and to stroke the newcomer's head. He was even more terrible than the former, and did not cease before cock-crow.

As the old song says:
In an old stone mortar
Where so many pestles have been, worn away,
There is need of a heavy copper hammer,
Or the work is lost.

At dawn, another bonze appeared and said to them in a low voice:

"Perhaps you have had your fill. Is not my turn coming?"

The first bonze gave a chuckle, but rose and went out. The other then got upon the bed, and very gently caressed the whole of Mei-chieh's body.

She pretended to repulse him, but he kissed her upon the lips, and said in her ear:

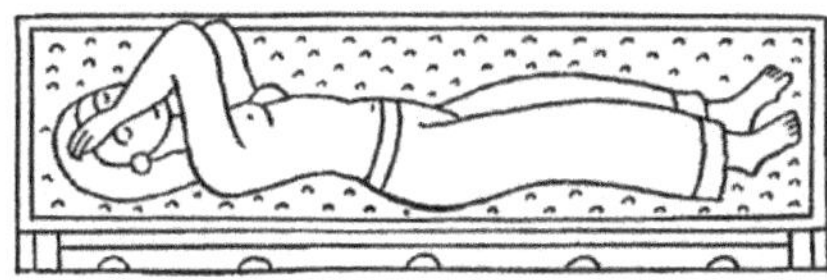

"If he has fatigued you, I have here some pills which will restore the Springtime of your thoughts."

And he thrust a pill into her mouth, which she could not avoid swallowing. A perfume rose from her mouth into her nostrils, and caused her bones to melt, imbuing her body with delicious warmth.

But, even while thinking of her own pleasure, Mei-chieh did not forget the Governor's orders. She marked the head of this new assailant also, saying:

"What a nice sleek old pate!"

The bonze burst out laughing:

"I am full of tender and reliable emotions. I am not like the unmannerly people of our town. Come and see me often."

And he retired.

Meanwhile the Governor had left his yamen by the fifth watch, before the day had yet broken, accompanied by an escort of about a hundred resolute men, carrying chains and manacles.

Arriving at the still closed gate of the monastery, he made the greater part of his train hide to the right and left, keeping only some ten men about him. The secretary knocked at the gate, crying that the Governor was there and wished to enter.

The first bonzes who heard his shout made haste to arrange their garments and receive the visitor. But the Lord Wang, paying no attention to their salutations, went straight to the apartment of the Superior, who was already, up and prepared to begin the ritual of his greeting. But the Governor dryly ordered him to summon all the bonzes, and to show him the Convent register.

Somewhat alarmed, the Superior ordered bells and drums to be sounded, and the bonzes, snatched from their sleep, ran up in groups. When the names written on the register had been called, the Governor commanded the astonished monks to remove their skull-caps.

In the full light of the morning sun three heads were seen to be marked with vermilion, but, Oh, prodigy, no less than eleven heads were covered with black ink!

"It no longer surprises me that these prayers should be so successful," murmured the secretary. "Indeed these bonzes are very conscientious!"

Lord Wang pointed out the guilty ones, and caused them to be put in chains, asking: "Whence come these marks of red and black upon you?"

But the kneeling monks looked at each other and could not answer, while the whole assembly remained stricken with wonder at this strange event.

Meanwhile the secretary had gone into the Babies' Chapel and, by dint of shouting, had roused the two harlots from a heavy sleep.

They quickly put on their garments, and came to kneel before the Governor, who asked them:

"What did you see during the night? Tell me the whole truth."

Since they had agreed to the mission, the two women rendered a plain account of the events of that night, showing the pills which the bonzes had given them, and also their boxes of vermilion and black.

The bonzes, seeing that their schemes were brought to light, felt their livers turn and their hearts put out of working. They groaned in their secret despair, while the fourteen culprits beat the earth with their brows and begged for mercy.

"Miserable wretches, you dare to preach divine intervention, so that you may deceive the foolish and outrage the virtuous! What have you to say?"

But the cunning Superior already had his plan. He ordered all the bonzes to kneel, and said:

"These unhappy ones whom you have convicted are without excuse. But they were the only ones who dared to act so. All my other monks are pure. You have been able to discover the shame of the guilty, which I in my ignorance could not, and there is nothing for it but to put them to death."

The Governor smiled:

"Then it is only the cells which these two women occupied that have secret passages?"

"There are only those two cells," answered the unblushing Superior.

"We shall question all the other women, and then see."

The female visitors, who had already been wakened by the noise, came in turns to give their evidence. They were all in agreement: no bonze had come to trouble them. But the Governor knew that shame would prevent them from speaking, and therefore had them searched. In the pocket of each was found a little packet of pills. He asked whence these came; but the women, purple in the face and scarlet in the neck, answered no word.

While this examination was taking place, the husbands of the penitents came up and took a part in it. And their anger made them tremble like the hemp-plant or leaves of a tree. When the Governor, who did not wish to push his questioning too far, had allowed the visitors to depart, their husbands swallowed their shame and indignation, and led them away.

The Superior had not yet given up the fight. He asserted that the pills had been given to the women as they entered the monastery. But the two harlots again affirmed that they at least had received them during the visit of the bonzes.

"The matter is quite clear," the Governor cried at length. "Put all these adulterers in chains!"

The bonzes had some thought of resisting; but they had no weapons and were outnumbered. The only ones left free were an old man who kindled the incense, and the two little novices still in childhood.

The gate of the monastery was closed and guarded. On his return to the yamen, the Governor took his seat in the Hall of Justice, and had his prisoners questioned in the usual ways. Fear of pain loosened their tongues, and they were condemned to death. They were cast into prison to await the ratification of their sentence.

As the Governor of the prison went his rounds to inspect their bonds, the Superior whispered to him:

"We have brought nothing, neither clothes, nor blankets, nor food. If you will allow me to return for a moment to the monastery with three or four of my monks, I will willingly give you a hundred ounces of silver."

The prison governor knew the wealth of the monastery. He smiled:

"My price is a hundred ounces for myself, and two hundred for my men."

The Superior made a grimace, but was compelled to promise this larger sum. The warders consulted with each other, and finally, when night came, led the Superior and three of his bonzes back to the monastery. From a secret place among their cells the monks took the promised three hundred ounces, and gave them at once to the warders. While these were weighing them and sharing them among themselves, they collected the rest of their treasure, and secretly laid hold of weapons, short swords and hatchets, which they rolled up in their blankets. Also they brought away wine. Thus heavily laden, warders and bonzes alike returned to the prison, and held a feast. The priests succeeded in making their warders drunk. In the middle of the night they drew forth their weapons and, having first set each other free, proceeded to force the gates. They might perhaps have escaped altogether; but in their rancour against the Governor they went first to attack the yamen.

The troops of police were numerous and well armed, and the bonzes were quickly overcome. The Superior gave his men orders to return as quickly as possible to the prison, to lay down their arms and to say that only a few of them had revolted, since this might save the others. But the warders attacked them so hotly that they were all put back in chains.

Their crime was grave, and doubly aggravated by rebellion. Next day, when the sun had well risen, the Governor gave his judgment. All the hundred and twelve monks were led straight to the market-place and beheaded. Groups of men provided with torches went to set fire to the monastery, and it was soon a smoking ruin. Joy flowered upon the faces of all the men of that town. But it is said that many of the women wept in secret.

Adapted from Hsing shih heng yen (1627), 39th Tale.

A COMPLICATED MARRIAGE

Marriages have from all time been arranged beforehand by Heaven. If such is the will of destiny, the most distantly separated persons come together, and the nearest neighbors never see each other. All is settled before birth, and every effort of mortals does but accomplish the decree of Fate. This is proved by the following story.

During the Ching-yu period of the Sung dynasty, there lived at Hang-chow a doctor named Liu. His wife had given him a son and a daughter. The son, who was but sixteen years old, had been called Virgin Diamond, and was betrothed to young Pearl, of the family of Sun. He was brilliant in his studies, and gave every promise that he would one day attain to the highest literary standard, and to the greatest honor. The daughter was named Prudence. She was fifteen years old, and had just received marriage gifts from her betrothed, the son of P'ei, a neighboring druggist. Her eyebrows were like the feelers of a butterfly, and her eyes had the grace of those of a phoenix. Her hips, flexible as willow branches swayed by the wind, wakened the liveliest feeling. Her face was that of a flower; and the nimbleness of her light body brought to mind the flight of swallows.

The go-between who had concluded Prudence's betrothal came one day at the instance of the P'ei family to ask that marriage might be hastened. But Liu had determined first to accomplish the ceremonies for his son, and accordingly took customary steps with this object in view, so that a day was at length fixed. But when the appointed time was drawing near, Virgin Diamond fell seriously ill. His father, Liu, wished to postpone the ceremony, but his mother argued that perhaps joy would cure him better than medicine.

"But if, by mischance, our son should die?" he insisted.

"We will send back the bride and all the gifts, and the family will have nothing to say."

The doctor, like many men, was wax in the hands of his wife, and therefore her wish was fulfilled.

But it chanced that one of their neighbors had been slightly affronted by them, and had never forgiven them. He heard of Virgin Diamond's illness, and spoke of it to the family of Sun.

Sun had no intention of compromising his daughter's future; so he summoned and questioned the go-between who had arranged the betrothal. The poor woman was in a great quandary, fearing to offend either the one family or the other; yet she was compelled to admit the truth. In her anxiety she ran to the house of Liu to obtain a postponement of the marriage until Virgin Diamond's recovery, and hinted that, failing this, Sun would send his old nurse to see the sick bridegroom.

Liu did not know what to do, and before he had come to a decision, the nurse arrived. He saluted her, not knowing what excuse to make. At last he said to the go-between: "Be so good as to entertain this venerable aunt for a moment, while I go and find my Old-Thornbush."

He hurried into the interior of the house, and in a few words told his wife what was happening.

"She is already here and wishes to see our son. I told you that it would have been better to change the day."

"You really are a decayed piece of goods. Their daughter has received our gifts, and is already our daughter-in-law. You shall see."

Then she said to Prudence:

"Make haste and prepare our large room for a collation to the family of Sun."

She herself went to the room where the nurse was, and asked:

"Has our new daughter's mother something to say to us?"

"She is uneasy about the health of your honorable son, and has sent me to see him, thinking that it would be better to postpone the marriage if he were seriously ill."

"I am gratified to receive this proof of her consideration. My son has, in fact, taken cold, but it is not a serious indisposition. As for choosing another day, that is not to be thought of. Our preparations are made, and a delay would involve too great a loss. Furthermore, happiness drives away every ill. The invitations are sent out. We might imagine that your family had changed its intention...."

"At least, can I see the invalid?"

"He has just taken a drug and is asleep. Besides, I have told you that he has caught cold. Are you trying to insult me by expressing a wish to prove my words?"

"If the matter stands thus," the nurse politely made haste to answer, "it only remains for me to withdraw."

"You cannot go in this way. You have not even taken a cup of tea. If you please, let us go into the new room, for my house is all in disorder."

On entering, the nurse observed the excellent arrangement of the young couple's apartment.

"Everything is ready, as you see," said the wife of Liu. "And if my son is not quite recovered after the ceremony, I shall take care of him in my pavilion, until he is able to embark upon his conjugal life."

Having taken tea, the nurse at last arose and went away. On her return she recounted to her master and mistress what had taken place, and Sun and his wife found themselves in a difficult dilemma. They could not think of allowing their daughter to ruin her life by entering of her betrothed, if he were going to die, and, if the young man were not seriously ill, they stood the risk of losing all their preparation, and of giving occasion for slander. Suddenly their son Yu-lang, who was present, said:

"If they have not allowed him to be seen, it means that he is seriously ill. There is no way by which we can go back on our contract; and yet we cannot send my sister to her ruin in this fashion. I have a plan, and you must tell me what you think of it. Let us send the go-between to advise Liu that the marriage will take place on the appointed day, but that the bride's equipment will not be sent until after her husband's recovery. I am sure that they will reject this offer, and then we shall have a good excuse for throwing the blame on them."

"But what if they should agree?" objected his parents, after a moment's reflection.

"They will certainly not agree, or else they would have postponed the marriage. Besides, it is impossible that they - should be willing to have another mouth to feed, without any dowry or plenishing."

His father said:

"Very well, if by any chance they do agree, you shall disguise yourself as a woman and go in your sister's place. You could take a man's clothing with you, and put it on if the sick youth recovered, or matters seemed to take an unfortunate turn. They would not dare to say anything for fear of being ridiculed."

"Oh! That is impossible!" cried the young man. "In the first place I would be discovered at once. And what would people say of me afterwards?"

"They would say that you had played a trick on these people, and that is all. You are still in the freshness of youth. You are sufficiently like your sister to deceive those who do not know you very well, especially in a wedding garment. You must do it. That is decided. The nurse can go with you to arrange your hair.... And in this way, if our son-in-law dies, Liu will have neither my daughter nor her equipment."

When the wife of Liu received Sun's proposal from the mouth of the go-between, she hesitated for a moment. But then she reflected on the false situation in which she would be placed by refusing. So, masking her thoughts beneath a smile, she agreed to the arrangement.

On the day fixed for the marriage, Yu-lang was constrained to disguise himself. But two grave difficulties presented themselves. First with regard to his feet: how was it possible for him to imitate his sister's ravishing golden lotuses, so like to sphinx heads, and the balancing of her light steps, a swaying of flowers in the soft breeze? They gave him a petticoat which reached to the ground, and he practised his sister's gait, at which she laughed until she cried. The next question was his ear-rings. It so happened that his left lobe had been pierced; for in his childhood they had made him wear one ring, in order to persuade the evil spirits that he was a girl, whose death would be of no importance. Everybody knows that the Jinn always endeavor to rob us of that which is truly dear to us, and leave untouched that which is of no value.

So Yu-lang hung a jewel in his left lobe, and stuck a small piece of plaster over his right ear, so that it might seem it had suffered a slight wound. His great pearl-decorated headdress concealed his head, brow and shoulders. His scarlet robes, embroidered with gold and silver, helped to disguise his figure, and the transformation was complete by rouge on his lips and cheeks.

When evening at length drew near, drums and flutes were sounded, the flowered palankeen entered the courtyard, and the hoodwinked go-between, admiring the beauty of the - bogus bride, herself opened the scarlet curtains. Not seeing Yu-lang, she remarked upon this circumstance, and they answered carelessly that he was indisposed and kept to his bed. Actually at that moment he was taking leave of his parents and imitating to the best of his ability the sobs which were fitting to the occasion.

The procession at last set out and all the bride's equipment was a little leather trunk. At the house of Liu there was considerable discussion:

"When the bride arrives, our son will be unable to cross the threshold as ritual demands, and the marriage will not be accomplished. The bride will be left alone to salute the ancestors, and this is impossible. What shall we do?"

"It cannot be helped," answered the mother. "So much the worse! Our daughter must make it known that she will take her brother's place. She shall recite the poem of the threshold in his name, and the rites will be thus observed."

And Prudence, in her graceful girl's garments, did in fact receive the false Pearl as she got out of the palankeen, pronounced the sacred formulas, and led the new bride before the tablets. The two seeming sisters-in-law knelt down, and several of the bystanders laughed inwardly to see two women perform the marriage ceremony, and then kneel for the purpose of the grand prostration.

The wife of Liu led Yu-lang to the invalid's bed; but he had been, excited and troubled by the music and noise, and had fainted. They had hastily to revive him by pouring some spoonfuls of hot soup in his mouth.

At length the false bride was led to the prepared pavilion, and her great veil was taken off. Then her fresh beauty shone forth, and everybody uttered exclamations of joy: the wife of Liu was alone in feeling a certain compassion, for she thought of all that the new bride would have to lose, and deplored her son's misfortune in falling ill at the moment of tasting so great happiness.

As for Yu-lang, the tedium of beholding the hideousness of all the guests was curiously diminished by the pleasure of seeing Prudence's delectable face. He thought:

"What a misfortune that I am already betrothed! Here is she whom Fate should have given me."

Prudence, on her part, felt herself drawn towards him in an irresistible manner, and said to her mother and the go-between:

"Alas! Surely my brother has no luck, and my sister-in-law will be very unhappy alone tonight! Is she not charming? If my future husband were like her, my life would be free from all regret."

Meanwhile, the marriage feast came to an end, a present was sent to the musicians, and the guests withdrew.

The disguised boy, after being conducted to his pavilion, had his nurse's -assistance in unmaking the complicated structure of his nuptial adornment. At last he found himself alone, but with no wish for sleep. Now Liu and his wife said to each other:

"It seems hard to leave the newly-wed bride alone for her first night under our roof. Would it not be better to tell Prudence to go and keep her company?

As always, the father made certain objections which were not listened to. Prudence insisted, and soon mother and daughter went together to the new pavilion, and approached the bed, the curtains of which were drawn shut.

"Here is your sister-in-law come to spend the night with you..."

Yu-lang did not know what to say. He was afraid of being discovered, and held the curtains very tightly under his chin, as he put his head through the opening.

"I am accustomed to be alone," he stammered. But the mother said:

"Aya! You are both of the same age, you are almost sisters.

What are you afraid of? If you want to be particular, you have only to keep a blanket between you."

During this time, Yu-lang was moved as much by fear as by delight. Was it not strangely fortunate that Prudence's mother should herself have come and let her in this manner to his bed? But if the young girl should call out? On the other hand he thought:

"She is fifteen years old, therefore she has been ready for some time; the door of her emotions is ajar. If I take precaution and kindle her heart little by little, there is no need to fear that she will refuse to nibble at my hook."

Now the wife of Liu had already retired, and Prudence had shot the bolt of the door. She was laughing all over the bright chrysanthemum of her face:

"Sister-in-law, you have taken no refreshment. Are you not hungry? If you wish for anything, tell me, and I will go and fetch it for you."

"I am deeply grateful to my sister-in-law for her gentle thought."

Prudence noticed that the wick of the lamp had not been trimmed, and was burning long, straight and red. So she exclaimed:

"That is for your happiness, sister-in-law!"

The other could not restrain a burst of laughter.

Prudence blushed and laughed also:

"You know how to be merry."

So they talked together. At length the maiden, taking the flowers out of her hair, got upon the bed and knelt down to undress herself. He asked her:

"On which pillow would you like to sleep? The lower one?"

"As my sister-in-law wishes."

"Then, if you please, let us sleep on the same."

"Very well."

Prudence had slipped under the blankets to finish undressing, and the boy did likewise, removing his upper garment, The lamp, placed on a little table beside the bed, dimly lit up the recess through the thin curtains.

His emotion began to rise, and he asked:

"How many flowering Springtides have you known?"

"Fifteen, this year."

"Are you betrothed?"

But she was seized with unaccountable shyness, and dared not answer. He brought his lips close to the delicate ear lying beside him, and whispered:

"Why are you so bashful? We are only two women together."

Very low, she answered him:

"I am betrothed to the son of P'ei, the druggist, and already they are urging that the ceremony should take place. Happily nothing is yet decided."

"You are not very eager, then?"

She pushed his head gently away, saying:

"It is not nice of you to take hold of my words in this way, and to make fun of me. If I am not eager, you do not seem to be any more so than I."

"And how do you know that, maiden? In any case, how could I be so when we are two women?" "You speak to me as if you were my mother," the other laughed.

"Considering my age, I should rather be your husband," he thoughtlessly said.

She burst out laughing:

"It is I who am the husband, seeing that I took my brother's place at the wedding."

"Well, let us not argue, but rather act as if we were husband and wife."

Thus both of them spoke words of meaning. They grew more and more passionate.

"Since we are husband and wife," he said impatiently, "why do we not sleep under the same blanket?"

As he spoke, he pushed back the thick quilt, and began to caress the upper part of her so sweet and smooth, so soft and graceful body. She had kept on an under garment, but her heart was filled with Springtime thoughts, and she offered no resistance to his hand.

Then, trembling with desire, he came to her breasts that had so lately dawned, and were so firm. Their tender points were red as a cock's crest, and in all things lovable.

Delighted with this game, Prudence put out her hands to return his caresses, and also found his breasts. But there was nothing but quite a little button. She was astonished, and said to herself:

"She is as tall as I am. How comes it that she is not further developed?"

But by this time Yu-lang was holding her right in his arms, and had his lips glued to hers, wantonly thrusting out his tongue. She continued the game by giving it a little nibble, and then thrust out her own tongue. This he so tenderly caressed with his that the girl's body seemed all at once to melt, and she said languorously:

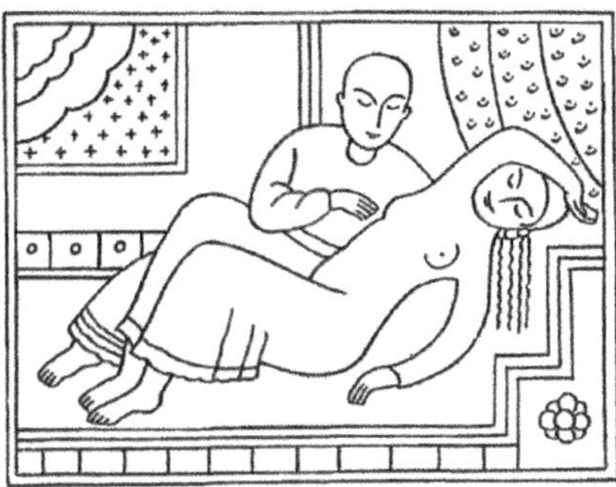

"This is no longer a game. We are truly husband and wife!"

The false bride, seeing that he had fully awakened the passion of his dupe, made answer:

"Not yet. We must take off our under garments."

"But I am afraid lest people should talk. It is not good to take them off."

He gave a nervous laugh and, without paying attention to her words, undid her girdle and took off her garment. As his finger advanced toward the secret, she protected herself with her two hands, saying:

"Sister-in-law, sister-in-law, you must not!"

But he kissed her again upon the lips.

"There is nothing to forbid it, little sister. You may caress me also."

In her agitation, and so as not to seem too stupid, she took off his vest, and her timid little hand suddenly encountered a certain matter. Her surprise was such that, for a moment, she could not speak. But at last she said: "What man are you who dare to take my sister-in-law's place?"

"I am your husband," he answered hugging her to him.

She pushed him off, and said seriously:

"If you do not tell me in plain truth who you are, I shall cry and call out, and you will be sorry for that."

"Do not be angry, little sister," he replied. "I will tell you everything. I am Yu-lang, your sister-in-law's elder brother. My parents heard that your brother was seriously ill, and did not wish my sister to leave our house; but since your parents would not alter the day of the marriage, I had to disguise myself and take my sister's place, until your brother should be healed. I never expected that Heaven would, in its bounty, allow me to become your husband. But we alone must know of our love. Let us not betray it to any."

Pressing forward again, he tried to bind her in his arms. Although she had believed she was with a woman, Prudence had loved him from the first; the feeling which she had mistaken for friendship quickly changed to that of love, for it was kindled, as was all of her, by the young man's ardour. Nevertheless she was suffused with shame, and so wavered between one extremity and the other.

As for him, in the freshness of his still maiden youth he spoke to her of everlasting vows, of a love higher than the mountain and vaster than the sea, and of a marriage shaped from a boundless happiness. Her betrothed, her parents and her shame were all forgotten. She covered her face with her hand and resisted no longer.

When the cloud and the rain of their intoxication had been dispelled, they clasped each other close and went to sleep.

Meanwhile, the nurse, being in the secret of this disguise, had been much disturbed at seeing Prudence share the young man's bed. From the adjoining room she had heard their laughter, and then their sighs, and had no further doubt of what had happened. And inwardly she cried: "Woe! Woe!"

In the morning, after Prudence had returned to her parents' house to perform her toilet, the woman came in to wait upon Yu-lang, and said to him in a low voice:

"O practitioner! You have done a fine thing! What will happen if people come to know of it?"

"I did not search her out. Her mother led her to my bed. How could I have avoided this?"

"You ought to have resisted with all your might."

"With an adorably beautiful girl in the same bed? Even a man of iron and stone could not have resisted. Also, if you say nothing, who will know of it?"

When the process of disguise was again completed, he went to salute the wife of Liu. Then all the women of the house and the cousins came to see him. Finally Prudence came in, and the two laughed together. For that day, as was the custom, Liu and his wife had invited their relations and friends, and there was a great feast, with music and a dinner lasting until the evening. Then, when the house was quiet again, the girl went, as on the previous night, to keep young Yu-lang company. That night, even more so than the preceding one, the butterflies beat their wings, and the passionate phoenixes were convulsed.

In the morning, they kept together. Therefore the scandalized nurse ran out and told everything to Sun and his wife, and they reeled with surprise and emotion.

"Alas, misfortune will certainly come of it! We must bring him back as soon as possible."

They summoned the go-between and told her that, according to custom, on the third day after the marriage they wished to see their daughter at their house. She therefore went to the home of Liu, and the two lovers trembled when they heard of this request. But the wife of Liu had not forgotten the difficulties which Sun had made with regard to the marriage; and she was afraid of not seeing her daughter-in-law again. So she said:

"But my son is still suffering, and the marriage has not been altogether accomplished. We will speak of this again at some later time."

This answer had to be sufficient. The nurse was in terror, and watched the approaches of the room all night for fear lest anybody should hear the rapturous exclamation of the lovers.

The days passed, and Virgin Diamond gradually grew better. Since he admired the beauty of his young wife, his desire to know her hastened his recovery, and the time came when he was able to get up. Still walking unsteadily, he went into the nuptial pavilion to see her who was his bride, and came before the door, supported by his attendants. The nurse was there, and cried out loud:

"My Lord wishes to enter!"

Yu-lang was, quite naturally, holding Prudence in his arms. He hastily released her, and went close to the door.

"You have succeeded in rising, my older brother?" said Prudence. "You will fatigue yourself."

"That is no matter," he answered, making a deep obeisance before her whom he believed to be his wife.

"Ten thousand happinesses be with you!" Yu-lang graciously replied.

"What an exquisite pair!" cried the wife of Liu, proud of her son and happy at his fortune.

The false bride's beauty was meanwhile strangely reviving the invalid's vitality. And the other lad thought:

"He is a fine boy in spite of his illness: there is no need to pity my sister. But if he can get up, he will waste no time in coming to spend the night with me. I must depart as quickly as possible."

When evening came, he explained his fears to Prudence.

"It is quite necessary to persuade your mother to send me back to my home, that I may change places with my sister. Everything will be discovered if we delay."

"You wish to go? But what will become of me alone?"

"I have already thought of that. Alas! Alas! But we are both betrothed to another. What can we do?"

"If you do not want me living, I must die so that my soul may follow you."

And she sobbed and sobbed. He dried her eyes saying to her:

"Do not meet trouble in this way, but leave me to find a plan."

They clasped each other in their arms, shedding most bitter tears.

Now it must be said that the wife of Liu was a little wearied of seeing her daughter night and day inseparable from her sister-in-law. However, she said nothing, because the marriage was not actually accomplished. But passing before the marriage pavilion on that day, she heard a sobbing. She drew near noiselessly and, through a hole in the window paper, saw them close in each other's arms and weeping.

"This is very odd," she said.

She wished to make an outcry, but remembered that her son was just getting better, and would fall ill again from any sorrow. She gently tried to push the door open, but it was locked. She called out:

"It is strange that this door should be locked!"

The lovers recognized her voice, and made haste to dry their tears and open the door. She came in.

"Why do you lock yourselves in during full daylight, and groan and embrace each other?"

They felt the blood flow to their faces, and answered nothing. The mother's hands and feet were trembling with rage. She seized hold of her daughter:

"You are playing some pretty trick. Let me talk to you a little."

And she dragged her into an empty room. The attendants who saw her asked each other why the girl was being dragged along like that. But by this time the mother had locked the door. When the attendants came and looked through the holes in the paper, they saw her lifting a stick, and heard her crying:

"O wretch, tell me the truth, or I shall strike you! Why were you weeping?"

At first Prudence thought of denial. Then she said to herself that it would be better to confess and to beg her parents to break off her betrothal with the family of P'ei, so that they might marry her to Yu-lang. If they refused, she would die. That was all. So she told the whole matter without evasion.

"We are husband and wife. Our love is boundless, and our vows will endure for at least a hundred years. My brother is recovered, and we fear that we shall be separated. Yu-lang wishes to return to his parents, to send his sister in his place. It seemed, then, to your daughter that a woman cannot have two husbands, and that if Yu-lang cannot marry me, I must die."

As she listened to her, her mother's breast opened with rage, and she stamped her feet: "This rotten carrion has sent his son here and has deceived me. And now my daughter is lost. I must beat him unmercifully!"

She seized her stick, opened the door and ran forth. Her daughter, forgetting her shame, tried to prevent her; but the old woman pushed her away violently, so that she fell down. Prudence got up and ran after her. The attendants also ran.

Now Yu-lang had very well understood that all was discovered when Liu's wife had dragged her daughter away. A moment later, the nurse hurried in.

"O my Gods! And, ah unhappiness! All is well lost! Prudence is being questioned with the stick."

It seemed to him that two knives were piercing his heart. He burst out into sobbing. But the nurse was already taking out his hair-pins and clothing him as a man. In a state of stupor he let himself be hurried to the main door and through the streets. A few moments later he was back at his parents' house.

His father did not fail to say to him:

"I told you to play the girl, not the man. Why have you committed acts of which Celestial Reason disapproves?"

Yu-lang jostled thus-by his father and his mother, no longer knew where he stood. Meanwhile the nurse objected:

"But what can they say there? Our young Lord has only to keep himself hidden for a few days, and it will all pass over."

But at Liu's house the nurse, as she went away, had unwittingly locked the door, and Liu's wife had come to it and was shaking it violently, stammering with rage and flourishing her stick.

"Thief, whom may Heaven strike dead! O very vile rascal! For what did you take me? I am going to show you who I am! I will have your life! If you do not open the door, I shall break it open with a great case."

But naturally no one answered. Prudence tried in vain to stay her mother, who loaded her with insults; but at last, in her rage, she succeeded in breaking the lock, and rushed into the room with her stick uplifted. The cage was empty and the bird had flown. She knelt on all fours to look under the bed and under the furniture, crying out all the time:

Thief, you shall die!"

But, as she was compelled to admit, there was no trace of the ravisher. Then Prudence said to her, sobbing meanwhile:

"And now, after this scandal, the P'ei family is let into the whole secret. I entreat you to have pity on me and let me marry Yu-lang. Otherwise, must I not die in order to redeem my shame?"

She fell on her knees, weeping and groaning.

"What you say is true," answered her mother, resuming some measure of calm. "After this wonderful affair, no one will want you."

However, a mother's love cannot be altogether restrained. She drew near to her daughter: "My poor child! All this is not your fault. It is that, rotten carrion of a Sun who has caused it. But we cannot, of ourselves, break off the betrothal with P'ei."

As Liu came up in the meantime, the matter had to be explained to him. He was nearly half a day without being able to speak, and it may be surmised that his first words were to throw the blame on his wife:

"The whole fault is yours! By making me say I do not know what, you arranged all this. Instead of altering the date as you should have done! And to crown all, you insisted upon placing our daughter in his arms! She has very well kept him company, has she not?"

His wife's anger was not quite dead, and these remarks rekindled it. Her voice rolled out like thunder:

"You old tortoise!" she began....

But on this occasion he also was furious. He advanced threatening to strike her. Prudence tried to come between them, and all three were nothing but a rolling, striking, shouting and weeping congeries. The servants then ran to inform Virgin Diamond who rose from his bed and unsteadily ran. His mother was moved with pity to see him, and his father also stopped his vituperation. They both went out muttering.

Virgin Diamond then asked his sister the cause of all this, and why his young wife was no longer there. She answered only with tears; but his mother, who had returned, told the whole story.

Virgin Diamond's anger was so strong that his face became the color of the earth. However, he contained himself, saying:

"Let us not publish this family shame abroad. If the news spreads, everybody will laugh at us."

As a matter of course, their mischievous neighbor, Li, had heard their shouting and weeping. He had quickly climbed on to his wall, but had been unable to understand what was happening. Next morning he watched for the first of the women slaves who came out, and drew her into his house. Fifty pieces of copper decided the girl to speak, and the delighted Li, letting her depart, ran to the house of P'ei, to whom he told all that he knew.

P'ei went straight to the house of Liu:

"I know all," he cried. "Give back the gifts, and let no more be said."

Liu's face became red and white by turns. He thought:

"How does he already know what happened in my house but yesterday?"

Then he denied the matter:

"Kinsman, whence come these words with which you are trying to sully my family?"

"Miserable cheat!" cried the other, "you are in very truth an old tortoise."

And he struck him on the face with his hand.

"Murderer!" cried Liu in a fury. "Do you dare to come to my house and insult me and strike me?"

And he struck P'ei such a violent blow that the old man fell to the ground. Then they began to belabor each other. Virgin Diamond and his mother, hearing their cries, ran up and separated them. Afterward P'ei, pointing with his finger and trembling, cried:

"You know how to strike, old tortoise! We shall see whether you are as clever in speaking before the judge."

And he went out swearing. Liu exclaimed:

"It is all Sun's fault. If I do not bring an action against them, they will even now escape entirely free."

In spite of his son's curses, he hurriedly set about writing an accusation, and ran to the Governor's palace.

The court was sitting, and Liu, holding his accusation, approached the judge. P'ei was already there, and reviled him as soon as he saw him. Liu retaliated, and the battle began anew.

At this interruption, the magistrate sternly ordered the two to kneel and explain themselves. Both spoke confusedly at the same time, but the whole story was none the less made clear. All those who were implicated in the matter were summoned, and they came to fall upon their knees.

At length the judge delivered sentence. All the former betrothals were annulled. Yu-lang became betrothed to her whom he had outraged. But the Sun family owed a compensation to the Liu family, which in its turn owed a bride to the P'ei family. So Pearl Sun was given to the son of P'ei, and Virgin Diamond was bestowed upon the former betrothed of Yu-lang. Having settled the affair, the Governor summoned three red palankeens and the three brides were conducted under escort to the homes of their new husbands. The town of Hang-chow talked of this affair for a long time, but in the end forgot it for some new scandal.

Hsing shih heng yen (1627), 8th Tale.

www.ingramcontent.com/pod-product-compliance
Lightning Source LLC
Chambersburg PA
CBHW070315190726
48291CB00013B/1577